STECK-VAUGHN

GAIN Essentials

English Skills Book 1

Steck-Vaughn®

HOUGHTON MIFFLIN HARCOURT

www.steckvaughn.com/adulted
800-289-4490

Printed in the U.S.A.

ISBN   978-0-547-52273-9

1 2 3 4 5 6 7 8 9 10   1689   19 18 17 16 15 14 13 12 11 10

4500263340   A B C D E F G

Table of Contents

Making Progress with Steck-Vaughn's
GAIN Essentials English Skills (Books 1–3)

The *GAIN Essentials* series is designed to provide you with the instruction and practice to master the GAIN Review Topics. This series will help you make progress toward your academic goals. The *GAIN Essentials* English Skills books focus on Reading, Grammar, Usage, and Style. Key features of these books include instruction and guided practice, as well as independent application, interactive learning strategies, and opportunities to connect what you learn to other situations and contexts.

Consistent Lesson Structure Enhances Mastery

Every lesson in the *GAIN Essentials* English Skills series uses the same format. This uniform structure enables you to gradually master each academic concept. As you become comfortable with the lesson setups, you'll know exactly what's coming next.

GAIN Learning Objective

This feature outlines the GAIN Review Topic(s) for each lesson in easy-to-understand language that allows you to preview the skills and concepts taught in each lesson.

Instruction

Using clear explanations and language, the instruction portion of each lesson teaches the target GAIN Review Topic(s) using real-world connections.

Understand It

This two-question section allows you to demonstrate your understanding of the instruction.

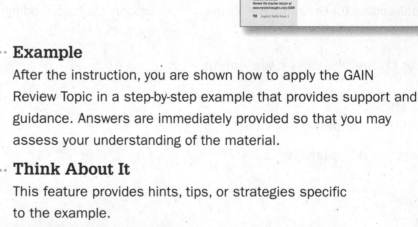

Example

After the instruction, you are shown how to apply the GAIN Review Topic in a step-by-step example that provides support and guidance. Answers are immediately provided so that you may assess your understanding of the material.

Think About It

This feature provides hints, tips, or strategies specific to the example.

Connected Learning

This feature demonstrates how the lessons in the book and the series are related and how they build depth of knowledge. You can see how each lesson supports material you have already learned and how each lesson prepares you for future lessons.

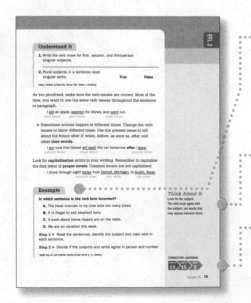

Try It

The *Try It* section provides guided practice with the GAIN Review Topic(s) from the instruction. Similar to the example, this feature uses condensed steps to provide more concise guidance. Answers are provided so you can independently assess your own understanding.

Before You Begin

This feature gives guidance or instruction about what you should consider before you begin work on the *Try It* problem.

Tips and Hints

Tips and Hints provide general notes about the *Try It* problems, as well as reminders about previously taught material or specific information to aid in the solution process.

 When you see this icon, you are encouraged to interact physically with the text of the *Try It* sections to help you focus on the task at hand.

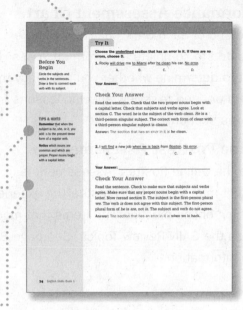

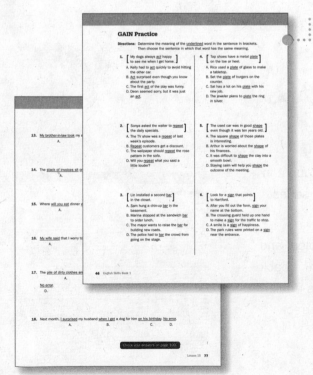

GAIN Practice

Once a GAIN Review Topic has been modeled and practiced, you are challenged to complete independent application. This allows you the opportunity to work with problems modeled after those on the actual GAIN. Answers and full explanations are provided at the back of the book.

GAIN Check In

The *GAIN Check Ins* allow you to assess your mastery of the GAIN Review Topics taught in the previous section of the book.

Performance Assessment Chart

At the end of each *GAIN Check In*, you are instructed to complete a Performance Assessment Chart to determine whether you are ready to move forward or need to review specific lessons from the previous section.

Online Posttest Assessment

While the Online Posttest Assessment is not timed, it mimics the GAIN test-taking experience by providing online practice with items that model and assess the GAIN Review Topics. See page 85 for more information.

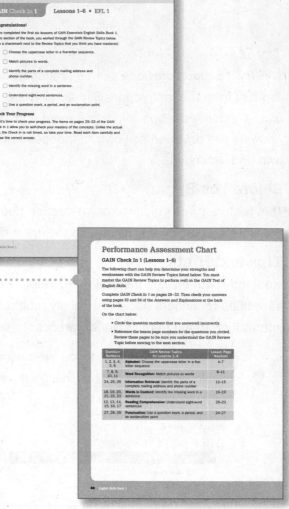

Resources and Support

Link to Online Posttest Assessment

This feature directs you to the Online Posttest Assessment, your next step toward GAIN success. See page 85 for more information.

Preview of the Next Book

This feature provides a sneak peak of the GAIN Review Topics taught in the next book, which provides the motivation to continue in the series.

Answers and Explanations

You can quickly check your answers for each *GAIN Practice* problem and *GAIN Check In* item in the *Answers and Explanations* section at the back of the book. This feature provides the correct answer, as well as a full explanation for why each answer choice is either correct or incorrect.

Addressing Your Instructional Needs

You have two options when using Steck-Vaughn's *GAIN Essentials* English Skills series.

> **1.** You may complete all lessons in order.
> **2.** You may create a customized study plan using the tables below.

You may choose to complete only the GAIN Review Topics suggested on your GAIN Individual Reports. After you complete the first form of the GAIN, you may use the *Instructional Needs* portion to decide which GAIN Review Topics to study. If you choose this option, you may place a checkmark next to every GAIN Review Topic below that appears on your GAIN Individual Report and study only those lessons.

This Appeared on My GAIN Report (✓)	GAIN Review Topics for EFL 1	I need to study...
	Alphabet: Choose the uppercase letter in five-letter sequence	Lesson 1
	Word Recognition: Match pictures to words	Lesson 2
	Information Retrieval: Identify the parts of a complete mailing address and phone number	Lesson 3
	Words in Context: Identify the missing word in a sentence	Lesson 4
	Reading Comprehension: Understand eight-word sentences	Lesson 5
	Punctuation: Use a question mark, a period, and an exclamation point	Lesson 6

This Appeared on My GAIN Report (✓)	GAIN Review Topics for EFL 2	I need to study...
	Reading Comprehension: Understand eight-word sentences	Lesson 7
	Words in Context: Identify the missing word in sentence	Lesson 8
	Words in Context: Understand the meanings of a word with multiple meanings	Lesson 9
	Charts: Retrieve information from a schedule	Lesson 10
	Capitalization: Capitalize the names of month and cities	Lesson 11
	Capitalization: Capitalize the title preceding a personal name	Lesson 11
	Punctuation: Use commas in a list	Lesson 12
	Verb Forms: Choose the correct form of a regular verb in the present tense	Lesson 13
	Verb Forms: Choose the correct form of an irregular verb in the present tense	Lesson 13
	Verb Forms: Choose the correct form of an irregular verb in the past tense and the future tense	Lesson 14
	Proofreading: Find and correct grammatical errors	Lesson 15

Wonderlic's General Assessment of Instructional Needs (GAIN)®

Wonderlic's General Assessment of Instructional Needs (GAIN)® is a new testing and scoring platform designed to assess English and math skills. GAIN is used by educational programs of all kinds, from post-secondary schools and adult basic education programs to literacy centers and workforce development programs.

Features that Set GAIN Apart

- **Detailed Reports** – The GAIN Report (see page x) provides a clear, graphical summary of English and math education levels and detailed diagnostics of a student's strengths and weaknesses. Comparisons between test scores are easy to read and understand.

- **Instructional Needs Are Provided** – Each GAIN Report suggests specific study and review topics, enabling students to close their learning gaps quickly.

- **45 Minutes Per Test** – Each test (English and math) takes a maximum of 45 minutes to administer. The *GAIN Test of English Skills* has 80 test items, and the *GAIN Test of Math Skills* has 75 test items.

- **One Test for All Levels** – The GAIN uses the same form to test all students, regardless of level. There is no locator test because there is no need to determine the educational level of each test-taker prior to administering the test.

- **Wonderlic Online** – When administered online, GAIN is automatically timed and scored with test results available within seconds. All test-taker data is stored in one location for simple student tracking and can be exported to another database.

- **Test Administrator Training and Certification** – Wonderlic provides free test administrator certification, along with ongoing training and support at no cost.

> ✳ **Approved by the U.S. Department of Education**
> GAIN has been approved for use in all NRS-funded Adult Basic Education programs.
>
> ✳ **Approved by the U.S. Department of Labor**
> GAIN has been approved for use in all Workforce Investment Act (WIA Youth) programs.

Steck-Vaughn's *GAIN Essentials*

Steck-Vaughn, long known as the gold standard in adult education, has created a new series that directly targets the GAIN Review Topics. Written with adult learners in mind, the approachable tone and accessible format present concepts in a way to which students can connect. Focus on the GAIN Review Topics allows content to remain tightly focused, and the *GAIN Essentials* books can be integrated into any student's study course.

Features that Set Steck-Vaughn's *GAIN Essentials* Apart

- **Links to GAIN's Review Topics** – Steck-Vaughn's GAIN Learning Objectives preview the GAIN Review Topic(s) taught in each lesson.

- **Focus on Student Needs** – Lesson format leads students through instruction with modeling and guided practice, ultimately preparing them for independent application. The lessons support independent study, but they can also be used in a group or classroom setting.

- **Self-Assessments** – Students are encouraged to check their progress as they move through the series. *GAIN Check Ins* allow students to identify their strengths and weaknesses.

- **Online Posttests** – At the end of each book, students will be directed to an online prescriptive posttest. The posttest mimics the look and feel of the actual GAIN.

- **Online Teacher Support** – There is one teacher lesson for every student lesson. The teacher lessons provide additional support, student activities, and extra practice.

- **Pacing Guide** – This feature allows instructors to award credit hours to each student based on their level of completion.

✳ **Easy for Instructors:** Steck-Vaughn's *GAIN Essentials* series can be easily integrated into current classroom curriculum.

✳ **Easy for Students:** Steck-Vaughn's *GAIN Essentials* lessons were designed with adult learners in mind.

Purchase the GAIN

Steck-Vaughn has proudly teamed with Wonderlic to distribute the GAIN. Please contact your Steck-Vaughn sales representative. You may also call our customer service team at 800-289-4490 or visit our website **www.steckvaughn.com/adulted**.

How Does the GAIN Work?

GAIN stands for General Assessment of Instructional Needs. It is published by Wonderlic, Inc. and assesses two subjects: English and math. GAIN is specifically designed to measure basic skills using the six Educational Functioning Levels (EFL) defined by the National Reporting System (NRS). The *GAIN Test of English Skills* is comprised of 80 assessment items and must be completed within 45 minutes.

The GAIN was developed to address the specific NRS EFL descriptors for each level. Scores for the GAIN are also reported in terms of those levels and provide individual feedback that pinpoints each student's instructional needs. This individualized scoring simplifies the process of placing students into classes that are appropriate for their skill abilities and ensures that students are assigned to the Steck-Vaughn *GAIN Essentials* book that addresses their individual learning needs.

GAIN English Score Range	EFL	GAIN Essentials English Skills
200–406	1	Book 1
407–525	2	Book 1
526–661	3	Book 2
662–746	4	Book 2
747–870	5	Book 3
871–1000	6	Book 3

Effectively Addressing Student Needs

After students take the GAIN, they will receive a report that details their strengths and weaknesses with the GAIN Review Topics. Students may then focus on those Review Topics listed in the *Instructional Needs* section of their individual GAIN Reports.

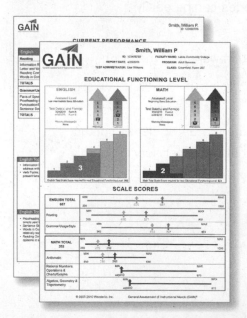

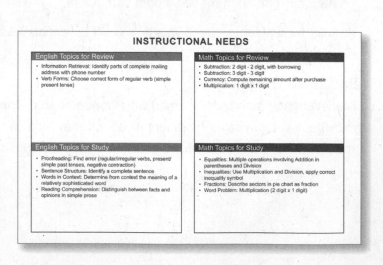

Using Steck-Vaughn's *GAIN Essentials* Series

The *GAIN Essentials* series is designed to help students make academic progress with the GAIN Review Topics, which are based on NRS Educational Functioning Levels (EFL). This six-book series was written with adult learners in mind and provides the instruction they need to master the skills and concepts for each EFL.

Placement within Series Based on GAIN Results

After students take the first form of the GAIN, they will receive a score report detailing their performance. Students and instructors may use this information to determine which book best meets a student's individual needs.

GAIN Essentials English Skills Book	Addresses the GAIN Review Topics at EFLs
1	1 and 2
2	3 and 4
3	5 and 6

Six Student Books

GAIN Essentials English Skills Book 1   *GAIN Essentials* Math Skills Book 1

GAIN Essentials English Skills Book 2   *GAIN Essentials* Math Skills Book 2

GAIN Essentials English Skills Book 3   *GAIN Essentials* Math Skills Book 3

Plus Online Assessments...

Online Posttest Assessment for English Skills Books 1–3

Online Posttest Assessment for Math Skills Books 1–3

...and Online Instructor Support!

Online Teacher Lessons for English Skills Books 1–3

Online Teacher Lessons for Math Skills Books 1–3

Plus pacing guides, correlations, and downloadable versions of the online posttest assessments

For online assessments and instructor support, please visit www.mysteckvaughn.com/GAIN.

Link to the National Reporting System

GAIN Essentials English Skills Book 1 addresses the GAIN Review Topics at Educational Functioning Levels (EFL) 1 and 2. According to the National Reporting System, students at EFL 1 can recognize, read, and write letters and numbers; can write a few basic sight words, as well as familiar words and phrases; may write simple sentences or phrases; and can write basic personal information. Students at EFL 2 can read simple material on familiar subjects and comprehend simple and compound sentences in single or linked paragraphs containing a familiar vocabulary; can write simple notes and messages on familiar situations; and can show some control of basic grammar and apply consistent use of punctuation.

Educational Functioning Level 1

This section of the book will teach the GAIN Review Topics for Educational Functioning Level 1.

Place a checkmark next to the topics you already know.

☐ **Alphabet:** Choose the uppercase letter in a five-letter sequence

☐ **Word Recognition:** Match pictures to words

☐ **Information Retrieval:** Identify the parts of a complete mailing address and phone number

☐ **Words in Context:** Identify the missing word in a sentence

☐ **Reading Comprehension:** Understand eight-word sentences

☐ **Punctuation:** Use a question mark, a period, and an exclamation point

GAIN
Learning Objective
In this lesson, you will learn about the order of the letters of the alphabet.

Uppercase Letters

All **words** are made up of **letters**. The **alphabet** has 26 letters. Each letter has two forms.

One form is called lowercase. **Lowercase letters** are used most of the time.

Lowercase Letters:

a b c d e f g h i j k l m n o p q r s t u v w x y z

S*he ate an apple*.
lowercase letters

Uppercase letters begin names. Use an uppercase letter to start a sentence. Uppercase letters are also called **capital letters**.

Uppercase Letters:

A B C D E F G H I J K L M N O P Q R S T U V W X Y Z

B*ob went to* **S***nake* **R***iver.*
uppercase letters

The letters of the alphabet are in order. The order is always the same. The letter *A* is first. The letter *Z* is last. This is called **alphabetical order.**

▶ Alphabetical order makes things easy to find. We file things in alphabetical order.

A*dams,* **J***ones,* **P***erry,* **S***anchez*
last names in alphabetical order

Look at the first letter of each last name. The letters are in alphabetical order: *A, J, P, S.* The names are in alphabetical order.

▶ Learn the letters of the alphabet in order. Start with *A*. Say five letters at a time: *A, B, C, D, E.* Then add five more. Do this until you can say the whole alphabet.

Understand It

1. The order of the alphabet is always the same.   **True**   **False**

2. The letters after the letter *V* are _____.

Teacher Reminder
Review the teacher lesson at www.mysteckvaughn.com/GAIN

Answers: True; W, X, Y, Z

Example

Put these words in alphabetical order.

Far

Hide

Ice

Goat

Step 1 ▶ Underline the first letter of each word. The words begin with *F*, *H*, *I*, and *G*.

Step 2 ▶ Say the alphabet. When you say *F*, write that letter. Keep saying the alphabet. Which letter comes next? *G* comes next. Write *G*. Keep saying the alphabet. Write the letters in the order that you say them: *F*, *G*, *H*, and *I*.

Step 3 ▶ List the words that begin with the letters *F*, *G*, *H*, and *I*.

Answer: Far, Goat, Hide, Ice

Try It

Choose the missing letter.

J K _?_ M N

  A. H

  B. I

  C. L

  D. O

Your answer: _____

Check Your Answer

The letters are in alphabetical order. One letter is missing. Say the alphabet out loud. Slow down when you get to *H* and *I*. The next letter is *J*. Say the letters after *J*. The first four letters after *J* are *K*, *L*, *M*, and *N*. Name the letter between *K* and *M*.

Answer: The correct letter is **L**.

Think About It

Think about the order of the letters in the alphabet.

Before You Begin

Review the uppercase letters of the alphabet.

TIPS & HINTS

Look at the two letters closest to the missing letter.

Try each of the answer choices to find the letter that belongs between *K* and *M*.

Write the alphabet. **Circle** the letters from the question.

CONNECTED LEARNING

LESSON 1 → LESSON 11

GAIN Practice

Directions: Choose the best answer.

1. F __?__ H I J
   A. E
   B. K
   C. G
   D. L

2. V W __?__ Y Z
   A. U
   B. A
   C. T
   D. X

3. L M N __?__ P
   A. O
   B. Q
   C. K
   D. R

4. __?__ C D E F
   A. G
   B. B
   C. Ł
   D. A

5. J K L M __?__
   A. I
   B. P
   C. O
   D. N

6. O P Q __?__ S
   A. T
   B. M
   C. R
   D. L

7. S __?__ U V W
   A. X
   B. Q
   C. T
   D. Z

8. N __?__ P Q R
   A. M
   B. S
   C. T
   D. O

9. ? I J K L

A. G

B. H

C. M

D. F

10. R S T ? V

A. U

B. Q

C. W

D. Y

11. E F ? H I

A. D

B. K

C. J

D. G

12. H I J K ?

A. G

B. L

C. M

D. E

13. V ? X Y Z

A. Q

B. U

C. W

D. T

14. B C ? E F

A. G

B. D

C. H

D. A

15. G H I ? K

A. J

B. C

C. F

D. L

16. P ? R S T

A. N

B. U

C. O

D. Q

Check your answers on page 90.

GAIN
Learning Objective
*In this lesson, you will
learn to match words
to pictures.*

Word Recognition

Words are made up of one or more **sounds**. The **letters** in a word tell
you the sounds.

Use letters and sounds to find the word that **names the picture.** Look
at the picture and say its name. Listen to the sounds at the beginning,
middle, and end of the word.

fork
barn
cane
corn

▶ Say the name of the picture. Listen for the **beginning sound.** The
words below have the same beginning sound. All of them start
with the letter *c*.

c̲up   c̲an   c̲ar   c̲ave

The letter *c* stands for the sound you hear at the beginning of the
name of the picture.

▶ Say the words below. Listen for the **middle sound.**

f̲or̲t   c̲or̲k   h̲or̲se   t̲or̲n

Each word has the same middle sound as the name of the
picture. The letters *or* stand for the sound you hear in the middle
of the name of the picture.

▶ Say the words below. Listen for the **ending sound.**

ca̲n   fi̲ne   hor̲n   ru̲n

Each word has the same ending sound as the name of the
picture. The letter *n* stands for the sound you hear at the end of
the name of the picture.

Say the name of the picture again. Look at the word choices. Think
about the beginning, middle, and ending sounds. The letters
c + *or* + *n* stand for those sounds. The word *corn* matches the picture.

Understand It

1. The letters in a word stand for _____.

2. The word *corn* has the same
   middle sound as *barn*.   **True**   **False**

Teacher Reminder
*Review the teacher lesson at
www.mysteckvaughn.com/GAIN*

Answers: sounds; False

Example

Which word matches this picture?

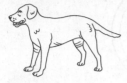

A. dot

B. bag

C. dig

D. dog

Step 1 ▶ Say the name of the picture. Listen to the beginning, middle, and ending sounds: d + o + g. Think about the letters that stand for those sounds.

Step 2 ▶ Look at each answer choice. Say the sounds that each letter stands for. Find the word that sounds the same as the word that names the picture.

Answer: D—dog

Think About It

Say the name of the picture out loud. Listen to the sounds you hear.

Try It

Choose the best answer.

PEPPER

A. **B.** **C.** **D.**

Your Answer: _____

Check Your Answer

Look at the word. The sounds in the word are "pep" and "er." Look at the pictures. Say the name of each picture. Only one picture names a word with the sounds "pep" and "er." The pictures name a pepper, tomato, desk, and paper.

Answer: The correct picture of a pepper is **A.**

Before You Begin

Say the word slowly. Look for letters you know. Think about the sounds they make.

TIPS & HINTS

Say the name of each picture. Listen to the sounds of the letters in each name.

CONNECTED LEARNING

GAIN Practice

Directions: Choose the best answer.

1.

   A. pin
   B. men
   C. pen
   D. pot

2.

   A. train
   B. truck
   C. tuck
   D. track

3.

   A. star
   B. farm
   C. stew
   D. sack

4.

   A. mitten
   B. jacket
   C. button
   D. bottle

5.

   A. arm
   B. eye
   C. ear
   D. deer

6.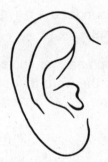

   A. belt
   B. barn
   C. ball
   D. bell

7. CHICKEN

A.

B.

C.

D.

8.

A. spin
B. melon
C. spoon
D. hoop

9. CLOCK

A.

B.

C.

D.

10.

A. snake
B. turtle
C. ankle
D. table

Check your answers on page 90.

GAIN
Learning Objective
In this lesson, you will learn to identify parts of a complete mailing address and phone number.

Addresses and Phone Numbers

A **mailing address** tells the **location** of a person or business. An address has three parts. It begins with the **name** of the person or business.

Manny Rico
name of person

The Paint Guys
name of business

The next line tells the **number of the building** and the **name of the street.**

Manny Rico
2010 Dock St.
building number and name of street

▶ Manny lives at 2010 Dock St. The letters *St.* stand for *Street.* A short form of a word is a called an **abbreviation.** You may see these abbreviations for kinds of streets: *Rd.* for *Road*; *Ave.* for *Avenue*, *Pl.* for *Place*; *Ct.* for *Court*; *Dr.* for *Drive*.

The last line tells the **city** and **state.** It also tells the **ZIP code.**

Manny Rico
2010 Dock St.
Dallas, TX 75201
city   state   ZIP code

▶ Manny lives in Dallas, Texas. Each state in the United States has an abbreviation. *TX* is the abbreviation for Texas.

The ZIP code is a number to help sort mail. It helps speed mail delivery. It tells the location of the address.

A **phone number** has ten numbers. The first three numbers are the **area code.** The area code tells an area in the United States.

(110) 555-1234
area code

The next seven numbers tell one person's phone number within the area code.

Understand It

1. What does an address tell you? _____

2. The area code of a phone number is the first three numbers.   **True**   **False**

Teacher Reminder
Review the teacher lesson at www.mysteckvaughn.com/GAIN

Answers: name of a person or business, building number, street name, city, state, and ZIP code; True

Example

Choose the best answer.

{
Ed Ospino
6924 Rock Rd.
Bakersfield, CA 93301
(661) 555-1234
}

Street Address?

A. Ed Ospino

B. 6924 Rock Rd.

C. Bakersfield

D. 93301

Step 1 ▶ Read the address and the question. The question asks you to choose the street address.

Step 2 ▶ Read each line of the address. Ed Ospino is the person who lives at the address. The street he lives on is Rock Road. Bakersfield is the name of the town or city. The ZIP code is 93301.

Answer: B—6924 Rock Rd.

Try It

Choose the best answer.

{
Vic Smith
334 Los Lobos Ln.
Winfield, TN 37892
(615) 555-1234
}

City?

A. TN

B. Vic Smith

C. Winfield

D. 334 Los Lobos Ln.

Your Answer: _____

Check Your Answer

The question asks you to name the city. The city is in Tennessee (TN). The city, state, and ZIP code are written on the same line.

Answer: The city is **Winfield.**

Think About It
Think about each part of an address. Decide which part tells the street address.

Before You Begin
Read the complete address. Identify the parts of the address.

TIPS & HINTS
Remember that numbers are used in the street address, ZIP code, and phone number. Each city is followed by the state's two-letter abbreviation.

CONNECTED LEARNING

LESSON 1 LESSON 3 LESSON 11

GAIN Practice

Directions: Choose the best answer.

1. { Anna Rios
446 Sundown Pl.
St. Louis, MO 63119
(314) 555-1234 }

Street Address?

A. Anna Rios
B. 446 Sundown Pl.
C. St. Louis
D. 63119

2. { Anna Rios
446 Sundown Pl.
St. Louis, MO 63119
(314) 555-1234 }

Name?

A. Anna Rios
B. 446 Sundown Pl.
C. St. Louis
D. 63119

3. { Anna Rios
446 Sundown Pl.
St. Louis, MO 63119
(314) 555-1234 }

City?

A. Anna Rios
B. 446 Sundown Pl.
C. St. Louis
D. 63119

4. { Tyrell Wilson
1325 Penn Ct.
Miami, FL 33173
(305) 555-1234 }

City?

A. Tyrell Wilson
B. 1325 Penn Ct.
C. Miami
D. 33173

5. { Tyrell Wilson
1325 Penn Ct.
Miami, FL 33173
(305) 555-1234 }

Street Address?

A. Tyrell Wilson
B. 1325 Penn Ct.
C. Miami
D. 33173

6. { Tyrell Wilson
1325 Penn Ct.
Miami, FL 33173
(305) 555-1234 }

Name?

A. Tyrell Wilson
B. 1325 Penn Ct.
C. Miami
D. 33173

7.

{ Elena Ochoa
4123 Dixon Dr.
Pittsburgh, PA 15219
(412) 555-1234 }

Name?

A. Elena Ochoa
B. 4123 Dixon Dr.
C. Pittsburgh
D. (412) 555-1234

8.

{ Elena Ochoa
4123 Dixon Dr.
Pittsburgh, PA 15219
(412) 555-1234 }

City?

A. Elena Ochoa
B. 4123 Dixon Dr.
C. Pittsburgh
D. (412) 555-1234

9.

{ Elena Ochoa
4123 Dixon Dr.
Pittsburgh, PA 15219
(412) 555-1234 }

Phone Number?

A. Elena Ochoa
B. 4123 Dixon Dr.
C. Pittsburgh
D. (412) 555-1234

10.

{ Richard McCloud
10023 Maple St.
Wilmington, DE 19893
(412) 555-1234 }

City?

A. Richard McCloud
B. 10023 Maple St.
C. Wilmington
D. 19893

11.

{ Richard McCloud
10023 Maple St.
Wilmington, DE 19893
(412) 555-1234 }

Name?

A. Richard McCloud
B. 10023 Maple St.
C. Wilmington
D. 19893

12.

{ Richard McCloud
10023 Maple St.
Wilmington, DE 19893
(412) 555-1234 }

Street Address?

A. Richard McCloud
B. 10023 Maple St.
C. Wilmington
D. 19893

Check your answers on page 91.

GAIN
Learning Objective
In this lesson, you will learn to name a missing word in a sentence.

Missing Words, Part 1

A **sentence** is made up of **words**. The words tell a **complete thought**. Each word is important.

> *The soup is hot.*

The words *The soup* tell what the sentence is about. The words *is hot* tell what the soup is like. "The soup is hot" is a complete thought.

You will see sentences like the one below on the GAIN.

> *The soup is ____?____.*
> deep   salty   hard

One word in the sentence is **missing**. That word tells what the soup is like. Look at the answer choices. The words *deep* and *hard* do not make sense. They do not describe soup. The word *salty* tells how the soup tastes. The soup is salty. The answer is *salty*.

▶ Every sentence has a word that tells what the sentence is about. Sometimes that word is missing.

> *My ____?____ is broken.*
> watch   sock   soup

The word that tells what is broken is missing. A sock can not be broken. Soup can not be broken. The answer is *watch*.

▶ Sometimes the action word in a sentence is missing. This word tells what happened.

> *Max ____?____ the football.*
> smiled   dressed   kicked

The sentence tells what Max did to the football. The action word is missing. Think about what you can do to a football. Read the answer choices. Which word tells what Max did to the football? It does not make sense to *dress* or *smile* a football. The best choice is *kicked*.

Understand It

1. The first word is the most important word in a sentence.   **True**   **False**

2. The words in a sentence tell a complete thought.   **True**   **False**

Teacher Reminder
Review the teacher lesson at
www.mysteckvaughn.com/GAIN

Answers: False; True

Example

Read the sentence. Which word is missing?

Bonita _____ the door.

- **A.** spilled
- **B.** walked
- **C.** closed
- **D.** cooked

Step 1 ▶ Read the sentence. Think about its meaning. The sentence is about Bonita, but a word is missing. The sentence does not tell a complete thought. It should tell what Bonita did to the door.

Step 2 ▶ Try each word in the sentence. Say the sentence. Which word tells what Bonita did to the door? It does not make sense that Bonita *spilled*, *walked*, or *cooked* the door. Bonita *closed* the door.

Answer: C—closed

Try It

Choose the best answer.

The train is _____.

- **A.** late
- **B.** sleepy
- **C.** happy
- **D.** soft

Your Answer: _____

Check Your Answer

Read the sentence. It is about a train. Think about the missing word. The missing word should tell about the train. What do you know about trains? Trains can be on time. Trains can be late. Trains cannot be sleepy, happy, or soft.

Answer: The best answer is **late.**

Think About It
Read the sentence. Think about what you can do to a door.

Before You Begin
Notice where the missing word comes in the sentence.

TIPS & HINTS
Think about words that can describe a train.

Try each answer choice in the sentence. Choose the one that makes sense.

CONNECTED LEARNING

LESSON 4   LESSON 8

GAIN Practice

Directions: Choose the best answer.

1. The flowers are ____?____.
   A. shy
   B. beautiful
   C. cold
   D. clean

2. The path was ____?____.
   A. narrow
   B. loud
   C. tall
   D. eager

3. We ____?____ a game.
   A. smelled
   B. walked
   C. turned
   D. played

4. The bus is ____?____.
   A. late
   B. proud
   C. dim
   D. tired

5. Her ____?____ is Kate.
   A. neck
   B. color
   C. name
   D. candy

6. The noise is ____?____.
   A. pink
   B. loud
   C. round
   D. hot

7. The _____?_____ is green.

   A. cloud

   B. dirt

   C. grass

   D. squirrel

10. Marta _____?_____ a cake.

   A. called

   B. closed

   C. baked

   D. hugged

8. The pool was _____?_____ .

   A. clever

   B. deep

   C. easy

   D. slow

11. My _____?_____ is brave.

   A. pocket

   B. brother

   C. bedroom

   D. hand

9. We _____?_____ the windows.

   A. folded

   B. kissed

   C. parked

   D. washed

12. Ellen _____?_____ the pail.

   A. melted

   B. smiled

   C. raked

   D. filled

Check your answers on page 91.

Short Sentences, Part 1

A **sentence** tells a **complete thought**. A sentence has two main parts. One part names a person, an animal, a place, or a thing. The other part tells what happens.

<u>Pam</u> <u>**rides the bus to work each day**</u>.
person   what happens

The first part of the sentence tells who or what the sentence is about. The word *Pam* names the person who is doing something. Pam is the **subject of the sentence.**

The second part of the sentence **tells what happens.** The words *rides the bus to work each day* tell what Pam does.

▶ Each word in a sentence tells you something.

The truck turned left at the stop sign.

The word *truck* names the thing that the sentence is about. *The truck* is the subject.

The word *turned* tells what happened. *Turned* tells what the truck did.

The word *left* tells how the truck turned. It *turned left. Left* tells the direction the truck went.

The words *at the stop sign* tell where the truck turned. When the truck came to the stop sign, it turned left.

▶ When you read a sentence, think about what each word tells. This will help you understand the meaning of the complete thought.

Understand It

1. A sentence has one main part.   **True**   **False**

2. A sentence tells a _____.

Teacher Reminder
Review the teacher lesson at
www.mysteckvaughn.com/GAIN

20 English Skills Book 1

Answers: False; complete thought

Example

Read the sentence. Choose the word that answers the question.

【Mateo drove his new car to the store.】

Who drove the car?

    A. Mateo

    B. new

    C. car

    D. store

Step 1 ▶ Find the two main parts of the sentence. The sentence is about Mateo. Then ask, "What did Mateo do?" He drove his new car to the store. The word *drove* tells what Mateo did. The word *car* tells what he drove. The words *to the store* tell where he drove.

Step 2 ▶ Read the sentence and question again. Name the person who drove the car.

Answer: A—Mateo

Think About It

Each word in a sentence tells something. Find the subject of the sentence. Decide what the subject does.

Try It

Choose the best answer.

【Carla played the piano for the quiet children.】

What did she play?

    A. Carla

    B. piano

    C. quiet

    D. children

Your Answer: _____

Check Your Answer

Read the sentence. The sentence is about Carla. The word *played* tells what Carla did. The word *piano* tells what she played. The words *for the quiet children* tells who was listening. Read the question again. It asks *what* she played.

Answer: The best answer is **piano.**

Before You Begin

Read the sentence. Be sure you understand how the words are related.

TIPS & HINTS

Remember that *played* is an action word. Look for the thing that was played.

Circle the word that names the subject of the sentence. **Underline** the part that tells what happened.

CONNECTED LEARNING

LESSON **5** > LESSON **7**

GAIN Practice

Directions: Choose the best answer.

1. { Donna dropped her travel bag onto the scale. }

   Who dropped it?

   A. Donna
   B. travel
   C. bag
   D. scale

2. { Mrs. Kim took her paycheck to the bank. }

   Who took it?

   A. Mrs. Kim
   B. took
   C. paycheck
   D. bank

3. { Juan rides his bike to work every day. }

   What does he ride?

   A. Juan
   B. bike
   C. work
   D. day

4. { Taylor paid her income taxes before the deadline. }

   Who paid them?

   A. income
   B. taxes
   C. deadline
   D. Taylor

5. { The cooks chopped green peppers for the salsa. }

   What did they chop?

   A. cooks
   B. green
   C. peppers
   D. salsa

6. { Three friends decided to join the army together. }

   Who decided to join?

   A. three
   B. friends
   C. army
   D. together

7. { A customer asked the server for more water. }

Who asked?

A. more
B. water
C. customer
D. server

8. { Bold explorers found interesting things along their route. }

Who found them?

A. bold
B. explorers
C. things
D. interesting

9. { Kateri takes her shopping bags to the store. }

Who takes them?

A. bags
B. Kateri
C. store
D. shopping

10. { Tamika set her alarm clock for six o'clock. }

What did she set?

A. Tamika
B. clock
C. six
D. o'clock

11. { The dog scratched the door to go outside. }

What did it scratch?

A. dog
B. to go
C. door
D. outside

12. { Peter keeps his power tools in the garage. }

Who keeps them?

A. garage
B. tools
C. power
D. Peter

Check your answers on page 92.

End Marks

A **sentence** tells a complete thought. Every sentence begins with a **capital letter.** Every sentence ends with an end mark. An **end mark** can be a period, a question mark, or an exclamation point.

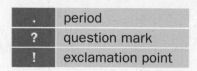

.	period
?	question mark
!	exclamation point

Use a **period** to end a sentence that **tells something** or **gives a command.**

She works in the garden.
tells something

Go work in the garden.
gives a command

Use a **question mark** to end a sentence that asks something. A question often begins with *Who, What, Why, When, Where,* or *How.* You can reply to, or answer, a question.

***What** is she planting in the garden?*
a reply is expected

▶ Some sentences look like questions, but they are not meant to be answered. This sentence begins with *How,* but it is not a question. The end mark can be a period or exclamation point.

How silly I was to lock my keys in the car!
a reply is not expected

Use an **exclamation point** to end a sentence that shows strong feelings. The example sentences above and below show excitement.

There is a ladybug in my coffee!
shows surprise

▶ End marks are one kind of **punctuation mark.** Other punctuation marks are used to separate ideas inside a sentence.

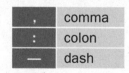

,	comma
:	colon
—	dash

This is my shopping list: milk, eggs, and bread—breakfast food.

Understand It

1. All sentences end with an end mark.   **True**   **False**

2. A question ends with an exclamation point.   **True**   **False**

Answers: True; False

Example

Choose the correct punctuation.

What color is your car _____

    A. .

    B. ,

    C. !

    D. ?

Step 1 ▶ Ask yourself, "Does the sentence tell something or give a command? Does it ask something? Does it show strong feelings?" The sentence asks a question. It begins with the word *What*. A reply to the question is expected. You could answer "My car is red" or "My car is blue."

Step 2 ▶ Ask yourself, "What end mark should I use for a question?" Look at the answer choices. Find the question mark.

Answer: D–?

Try It

Choose the correct punctuation.

How was Marco's job interview _____

    A. .

    B. ,

    C. !

    D. ?

Your Answer: _____

Check Your Answer

The sentence begins with the word *How*. The sentence asks about Marco's job interview. A reply to the question is expected. You could answer, "It was great!" A question mark is the end mark for a question.

Answer: The correct punctuation is (**?**).

Think About It
There are only three kinds of end marks: a period, a question mark, and an exclamation point.

Before You Begin
Next to each end mark, write its purpose.

TIPS & HINTS
Remember that a question needs an answer or reply.

CONNECTED LEARNING

LESSON 5 > LESSON 6 > LESSON 12

GAIN Practice

Directions: Choose the correct punctuation.

1. Where is the book _____
   - A. .
   - B. ,
   - C. !
   - D. ?

2. What is your name _____
   - A. .
   - B. ,
   - C. !
   - D. ?

3. Maddie was on time for work _____
   - A. .
   - B. ,
   - C. !
   - D. ?

4. Who will drive the van _____
   - A. .
   - B. ,
   - C. !
   - D. ?

5. Look out _____
   - A. .
   - B. ,
   - C. !
   - D. ?

6. When did you put gas in the car _____
   - A. .
   - B. ,
   - C. !
   - D. ?

7. Jared shut his eyes _____
   - A. .
   - B. ,
   - C. !
   - D. ?

8. Call 911 right now _____
   - A. .
   - B. ,
   - C. !
   - D. ?

9. How many eggs are in a dozen _____

A. .

B. ,

C. !

D. ?

10. Carlos bought a gallon of milk _____

A. .

B. ,

C. !

D. ?

11. Did slugs eat the corn in your garden ___

A. .

B. ,

C. !

D. ?

12. Who wants to order lunch _____

A. .

B. ,

C. !

D. ?

13. Please go and get the mail _____

A. .

B. ,

C. !

D. ?

14. Are we there yet _____

A. .

B. ,

C. !

D. ?

15. Where are the men playing soccer _____

A. .

B. ,

C. !

D. ?

16. Grab your keys before you go _____

A. .

B. ,

C. !

D. ?

Check your answers on page 92.

Congratulations!

You've completed the first six lessons of *GAIN Essentials* English Skills Book 1. In this section of the book, you worked through the GAIN Review Topics below. Place a checkmark next to the Review Topics that you think you have mastered:

☐ Choose the uppercase letter in a five-letter sequence.

☐ Match pictures to words.

☐ Identify the parts of a complete mailing address and phone number.

☐ Identify the missing word in a sentence.

☐ Understand eight-word sentences.

☐ Use a question mark, a period, and an exclamation point.

Check Your Progress

Now it's time to check your progress. The items on pages 29–33 of the *GAIN Check In 1* allow you to self-check your mastery of the concepts. Unlike the actual GAIN, the *Check In* is not timed, so take your time. Read each item carefully and choose the correct answer.

Directions: Choose the best answer.

1. C D _____ F G
   A. B
   B. H
   C. E
   D. M

2. J _____ L M N
   A. H
   B. C
   C. O
   D. K

3. V W X _____ Z
   A. S
   B. Y
   C. U
   D. Q

4. Q R S _____ U
   A. T
   B. P
   C. X
   D. V

5. N O _____ Q R
   A. M
   B. P
   C. S
   D. L

6. H I _____ K L
   A. C
   B. J
   C. D
   D. G

Continued on next page ▶

GAIN Check In 1 *continued*

Directions: Choose the best answer.

7.

A. sock
B. lock
C. land
D. rock

8.

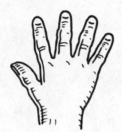

A. hand
B. sand
C. hall
D. hood

9.

A. ladder
B. butter
C. dinner
D. lemon

10.

A. bead
B. bear
C. bird
D. bean

11. TIGER

A.

B.

C.

D.

Directions: Choose the best answer.

12. { The teacher gave the student a new book. }

Who gave it?

A. student
B. book
C. teacher
D. new

15. { Alice stored the clean towels in the closet. }

What did she store?

A. towels
B. closet
C. Alice
D. clean

13. { Kent made a peach pie for his wife. }

What did he make?

A. wife
B. Kent
C. peach
D. pie

16. { Manuel listened to the radio with his earphones. }

Who listened?

A. radio
B. Manuel
C. earphones
D. his

14. { Brianna left her keys in her coat pocket. }

Who left them?

A. keys
B. pocket
C. coat
D. Brianna

17. { The neighbors worked together to clean the park. }

Who worked?

A. neighbors
B. together
C. clean
D. park

Continued on next page ▶

GAIN Check In 1 *continued*

Directions: Choose the best answer.

18. Abby fed her _____.
    - A. purse
    - B. dog
    - C. house
    - D. beach

19. The _____ goes fast.
    - A. car
    - B. shoe
    - C. chair
    - D. lamp

20. The snow is _____.
    - A. hot
    - B. sad
    - C. cold
    - D. tired

21. Anisha sang a _____.
    - A. lunch
    - B. garage
    - C. meal
    - D. song

22. Sam locked the _____.
    - A. brush
    - B. toolbox
    - C. flowerpot
    - D. jacket

23. The _____ is broken.
    - A. sock
    - B. food
    - C. glass
    - D. sun

24.

{
Anthony Hernandez
5685 Pearl St.
Nashville, TN 37201
(615) 555-1234
}

Street Address?

A. Anthony Hernandez
B. 5685 Pearl St.
C. Nashville
D. 37201

25.

{
Anthony Hernandez
5685 Pearl St.
Nashville, TN 37201
(615) 555-1234
}

Name?

A. Anthony Hernandez
B. 5685 Pearl St.
C. Nashville
D. 37201

26.

{
Anthony Hernandez
5685 Pearl St.
Nashville, TN 37201
(615) 555-1234
}

City?

A. Anthony Hernandez
B. 5685 Pearl St.
C. Nashville
D. 37201

Directions: Choose the correct punctuation.

27. What did Rosa have for lunch _____

    A. .
    B. ,
    C. !
    D. ?

28. The truck is in the garage _____

    A. .
    B. ,
    C. !
    D. ?

29. Where are the lightbulbs _____

    A. .
    B. ,
    C. !
    D. ?

Check Your Answers

Now that you've completed GAIN Check In 1, check your answers on page 93.
Then complete the Performance Assessment Chart on page 88. This will help you
determine whether you need to review any lessons or are ready to move to the next
section. Did you master all the concepts you checked on page 28?

Educational Functioning Level 2

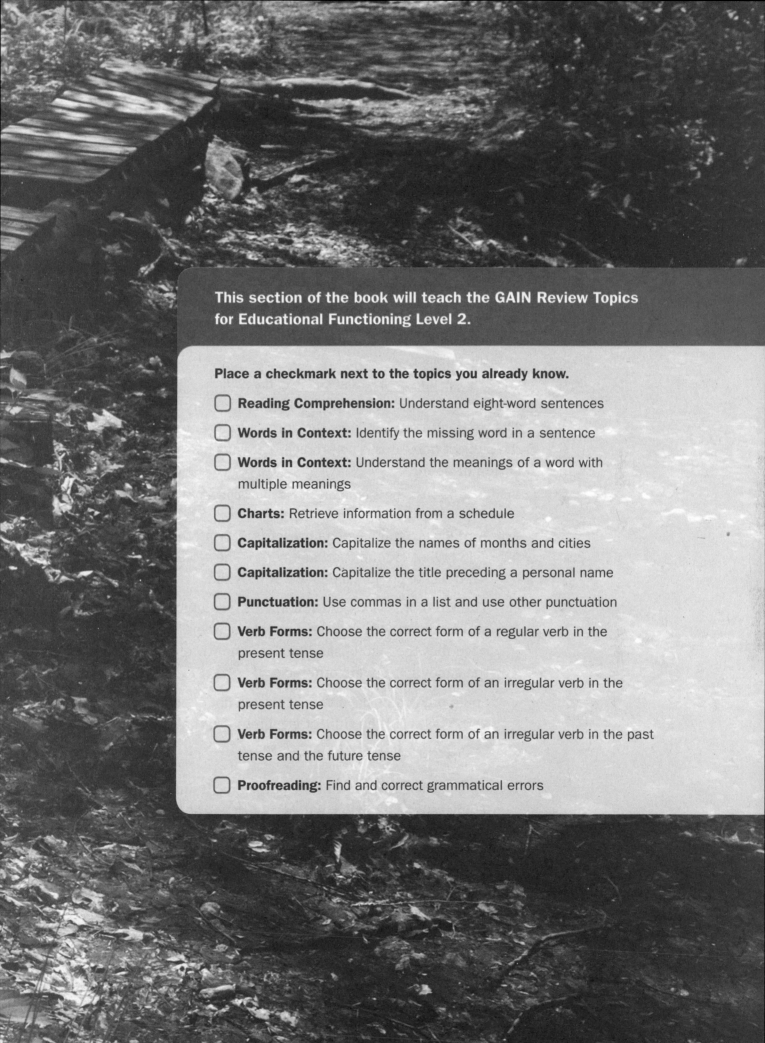

This section of the book will teach the GAIN Review Topics for Educational Functioning Level 2.

Place a checkmark next to the topics you already know.

- [ ] **Reading Comprehension:** Understand eight-word sentences
- [ ] **Words in Context:** Identify the missing word in a sentence
- [ ] **Words in Context:** Understand the meanings of a word with multiple meanings
- [ ] **Charts:** Retrieve information from a schedule
- [ ] **Capitalization:** Capitalize the names of months and cities
- [ ] **Capitalization:** Capitalize the title preceding a personal name
- [ ] **Punctuation:** Use commas in a list and use other punctuation
- [ ] **Verb Forms:** Choose the correct form of a regular verb in the present tense
- [ ] **Verb Forms:** Choose the correct form of an irregular verb in the present tense
- [ ] **Verb Forms:** Choose the correct form of an irregular verb in the past tense and the future tense
- [ ] **Proofreading:** Find and correct grammatical errors

Short Sentences, Part 2

A **sentence** is a group of words that tells a **complete thought**. A sentence has two parts: a subject and a predicate.

> <u>Jacob</u> <u>**repaired the leaky faucet in the kitchen**</u>.
> subject   predicate

The **subject** is often found at the beginning of a sentence. The subject is usually a **noun**. It names the person, animal, place, or thing that the sentence is about.

▶ To find the subject, ask, "Who repaired the faucet?" Jacob repaired the faucet, so *Jacob* is the subject.

Find the subject of the sentence below. Ask, "What made rust stains in the sink?" The water made rust stains, so *The water* is the subject.

> <u>*The water*</u> <u>**made rust stains in the sink**</u>.
> subject   predicate

The **predicate** often follows the subject in a sentence. It tells what the subject *does* or *is*. The predicate always has a word that **shows action or being**.

> <u>*The customers*</u> <u>**ordered club sandwiches for lunch**</u>.
> subject   predicate

▶ A predicate can have many words. To find the predicate, ask, "What did the customers do?" The words *ordered club sandwiches for lunch* tells what they did.

The word *ordered* is the action word, or a type of **verb.** The word *sandwiches* tells what the customers ordered. The word *club* describes the kind of sandwiches. The words *for lunch* tell when the sandwiches were ordered.

Some predicates have verbs that are not action words. These verbs tell what the subject *is* instead of what the subject *does*.

> <u>*Liam*</u> <u>**is a server at the snack shop**</u>.
> subject   predicate

This predicate tells what the subject *is*. It links *server* with *Liam*. Think of *is* as an equal sign (=): Liam = a server.

Understand It

1. The subject of a sentence names a person, an animal, a place, or a thing.   **True**   **False**

2. The predicate always has an action word.   **True**   **False**

Answers: True; False

Example

Read the sentence. Choose the word that answers the question.

[The carpenters build new homes in the city.]

Who builds them?

    A. carpenters

    B. new

    C. homes

    D. city

Step 1 ► Find the subject of the sentence by asking, "Who or what is the sentence about?" The sentence is about the carpenters. Find the predicate by asking, "What do the carpenters do?" They build new homes in the city. The action word is *build.* The word *homes* tells what they build, and *new* describes the homes. The words *in the city* tell where they build the homes.

Step 2 ► Read the question again, "Who builds them?" *Who* refers to the carpenters. The word *builds* tells what the carpenters do. The word *them* refers to the new homes in the city. The question asks, "Who builds new homes in the city?"

Answer: A—carpenters

Try It

Choose the best answer.

[The reporters researched facts for a newspaper article.]

What did they research?

    A. reporters

    B. newspaper

    C. facts

    D. article

Your Answer: _____

Check Your Answer

The subject of the sentence is *The reporters.* The action word is *researched.* The question asks, "What did the reporters research?" They researched facts for a newspaper article.

Answer: The best answer is **facts.**

Think About It
The question asks for the subject of the sentence. Remember that subjects are usually nouns that tell who or what did something.

Before You Begin
Underline the subject of the sentence and circle the action word.

TIPS & HINTS
Notice that the words "for a newspaper article" tell why the reporters are researching facts.

CONNECTED LEARNING
LESSON 5 > LESSON 7 > BOOK 8

GAIN Practice

Directions: Choose the best answer.

1. { Tess left her blue
     sweater on the bus. }

   Who left it?

   A. Tess
   B. blue
   C. sweater
   D. bus

2. { Jesse wrote a check
     for the auto repairs. }

   Who wrote it?

   A. repairs
   B. auto
   C. check
   D. Jesse

3. { The water pitcher slipped
     out of Amanda's hands. }

   What slipped?

   A. water
   B. pitcher
   C. hands
   D. Amanda's

4. { My brother bought two
     tickets for the concert. }

   What did he buy?

   A. brother
   B. two
   C. tickets
   D. concert

5. { George took a brisk
     walk around the block. }

   Who took it?

   A. George
   B. brisk
   C. walk
   D. block

6. { Keisha discovered a slow
     leak in her tire. }

   What did she discover?

   A. Keisha
   B. slow
   C. leak
   D. tire

7. { Dr. Abrams reviewed x-rays of my injured ankle. }

Who reviewed them?

A. Dr. Abrams
B. x-rays
C. injured
D. ankle

10. { The workers fixed the broken sidewalk with cement. }

Who fixed it?

A. workers
B. broken
C. sidewalk
D. cement

8. { Sylvie mixed chopped walnuts into the cookie dough. }

What did she do?

A. Sylvie
B. mixed
C. walnuts
D. cookie

11. { Squirrels climb the tall tree in our yard. }

What do they climb?

A. squirrels
B. tall
C. tree
D. yard

9. { Jared explored the history museum with his sons. }

What did he explore?

A. Jared
B. history
C. museum
D. sons

12. { Emil added some tomatoes to the beef stew. }

What did he add?

A. Emil
B. tomatoes
C. beef
D. stew

Check your answers on page 94.

GAIN
Learning Objective
In this lesson, you will learn to identify a missing word in a sentence.

Missing Words, Part 2

Sometimes on a test you will need to **complete a sentence** that has a **missing word.**

> **Which word best completes the sentence?**
>
> *Josh listens to Julia because he is a __?__ husband.*
>
> selfish   caring   serious

Read the sentence and think about its **meaning.** The missing word describes Julia's husband. What kind of person is Josh? The sentence says that he listens. You would not describe a person who listens as selfish. While the word *serious* may describe Josh, you cannot determine that from the information given. A person who listens is caring. The word *caring* best describes Julia's husband.

When you read a sentence with a missing word, look at the surrounding words for **clues** to the meaning of the word.

> *Angela reached her goal and was __?__ to store manager.*
>
> *promoted*   *discovered*   *stretched*

The words *reached her goal* tell you that Angela was successful. When you are successful, you can move up to a higher position. The word *promoted* means "moved to a higher level."

► Sometimes more than one word makes sense in the sentence. Look for clues that help you make **the best choice.**

> *If you are a __?__ person, people can depend on you.*
>
> *likable*   *clever*   *reliable*

The missing word describes a person that people can depend on. The words *likeable* and *clever* can describe a person, but only *reliable* means "can be depended on." *Reliable* is the best choice.

► A sentence may give **examples** of the missing word. Examples often begin with *like, such as,* or *for example.*

> *__?__, such as beets, peas, and carrots, are healthful foods.*
>
> *Fruit*   *Vegetables*   *Tomatoes*

The words *such as* tell you that beets, peas, and carrots are examples of the missing word. They are examples of vegetables.

Understand It

1. When you read a sentence, think about its _____.

2. You can get clues to a missing word
   from other words in the sentence.   **True**   **False**

Teacher Reminder
Review the teacher lesson at
www.mysteckvaughn.com/GAIN

Answers: meaning; True

Example

Which word best completes the sentence?

The Parks Department __?__ with the parents' group to build a playground and a nature center.

    A. argued

    B. cooperated

    C. invented

    D. completed

Step 1 ► Read the sentence and think about its meaning. The sentence is about two groups of people and what they did together.

Step 2 ► The sentence names two projects that the Parks Department completed—a playground and a nature center. Notice the words *with the parents' group.* This tells you that one group did not work alone. The missing word means "worked together." Read the answer choices. *Argued, invented,* and *completed* do not mean "worked together."

Answer: B—cooperated

Think About It
Think about the meaning of each answer choice.

Try It

Choose the word that best completes the sentence.

Anika fell down three stairs and __?__ her ankle.

    A. upset

    B. offended

    C. shook

    D. injured

Your Answer: _____

Check Your Answer

Look for words that give clues to the meaning of the missing word. The sentence says that Anika fell down the stairs. Something happened to Anika's ankle. Anika must have hurt her ankle when she fell. Look at the answer choices for a word that means "hurt."

Answer: The word that best completes the sentence is **injured.**

Before You Begin
Read the sentence to get a sense of its meaning.

Underline words that give clues to the missing word.

CONNECTED LEARNING

LESSON 4   LESSON 8   LESSON 9

GAIN Practice

Directions: Choose the word that best completes the sentence.

1. Can you smell the lovely __?__ of the candle?

   A. glow
   B. scent
   C. shade
   D. stink

2. I am beginning to __?__ because I can't find my bike on the rack.

   A. clash
   B. struggle
   C. panic
   D. relax

3. If Ed forgets to ice his ankle, it will continue to __?__ .

   A. shrink
   B. scratch
   C. swell
   D. improve

4. I am afraid of water, so I feel __?__ when I drive over a bridge.

   A. angry
   B. confused
   C. comfortable
   D. uneasy

5. You will do better on the test if you __?__ and study hard.

   A. forget
   B. prepare
   C. swallow
   D. revolt

6. Everyone should see the Grand Canyon to __?__ its beauty.

   A. experience
   B. exchange
   C. imitate
   D. spoil

7. My son is __?__, but my daughter is easy to please.

   A. friendly
   B. fussy
   C. clumsy
   D. eager

8. If you __?__ Ralph in the game, he can play first base.

   A. capture
   B. upset
   C. include
   D. believe

9. My brothers often __?__ about which sports team is best.

   A. check
   B. practice
   C. score
   D. debate

10. When the mayor said that the factory was closing, a __?__ was heard from the astonished crowd.

    A. whisper
    B. gasp
    C. squawk
    D. signal

11. The truck drove through a snowstorm and slid on the __?__ road.

    A. dusty
    B. bumpy
    C. icy
    D. rocky

12. The cell phone company tried to __?__ the quality of its service.

    A. improve
    B. collect
    C. interrupt
    D. require

Check your answers on page 95.

Multiple-Meaning Words

Some words have **more than one meaning**. The meaning of a word depends on how it is used in a sentence. Notice if the word names or describes something or if it is an action word. Then look at the surrounding words for **clues** to what the word might mean.

▶ The word *cover* has multiple meanings.

The newspaper sent a reporter to <u>cover</u> the election.

The word *cover* is an action word. It means "to report on an event." The words *newspaper* and *reporter* are clues.

The hikers took <u>cover</u> in a cave during the storm.

In the above sentence, *cover* names something means "shelter." The words *in a cave* and *during the storm* give clues to its meaning. Hikers would find shelter in a storm.

Marnie put a plastic <u>cover</u> on the couch to keep it clean.

Here the word *cover* names a thing you put over an object or person. A cover is placed over the couch to protect it from dirt and spills. The words *plastic, couch,* and *keep it clean* are clues to its meaning.

My paycheck will <u>cover</u> the groceries, but not the cable bill.

In this sentence, *cover* is an action word. It means "to provide enough." The paycheck provides enough money to buy groceries. It does not provide enough money to pay the cable bill.

▶ Which of the four examples of *cover* shown above is most like the following sentence?

The amount on the gift card will <u>cover</u> our dinners and the tip.

The gift card will provide enough money to pay for the meal and the tip. This is most like the meaning of *cover* in the fourth sentence: *My paycheck will cover the groceries, but not the cable bill.*

Understand It

1. The only way to learn the meaning of a word is to look in the dictionary.   **True**   **False**

2. Knowing how a word is used in a sentence can help you find its meaning.   **True**   **False**

Teacher Reminder
Review the teacher lesson at
www.mysteckvaughn.com/GAIN

44 English Skills Book 1

Answers: False; True

Example

Choose the meaning of *charge* that fits the sentence below.

Chin Ho gets a <u>charge</u> out of going to stock car races.

    A. the price of something

    B. thrill or excitement

    C. to attack by rushing forward

    D. an amount of electricity

Step 1 ▶ Think about the meaning of the sentence. Chin Ho reacts in some way to going to stock car races. He gets a *charge* when he goes to the races.

Step 2 ▶ Read the answer choices carefully. Decide which meaning of *charge* is something that Chin Ho is likely to feel at a car race. He is likely to be thrilled or excited.

Answer: B—thrill or excitement

Think About It
Tell the meaning of the sentence in your own words.

Try It

Determine the meaning of the <u>underlined</u> word in the sentence in brackets. Then choose the sentence in which that word has the same meaning.

[George sold his car and bought a newer <u>model</u>.]

    A. Can you <u>model</u> how to install a light switch?

    B. The <u>model</u> wore a black dress with red shoes.

    C. This <u>model</u> costs more than the other ovens.

    D. This toy is a <u>model</u> of my grandfather's first car.

Your Answer: _____

Before You Begin
Repeat the directions using your own words.

Write the meaning of *model* after each answer choice.

Check Your Answer

Look at the sentence in brackets. Think about the meaning of *model*. The word names something that replaced George's old car. In this sentence, *model* means "type" or "style." The sentence states that George bought a newer type of car. Read through the answer choices. Look for a sentence that uses *model* to mean a type or style of a product.

Answer: The correct sentence is **This <u>model</u> costs more than the other ovens.**

CONNECTED LEARNING

LESSON **9** BOOK **2**

GAIN Practice

Directions: Determine the meaning of the <u>underlined</u> word in the sentence in brackets. Then choose the sentence in which that word has the same meaning.

1. [My dogs always <u>act</u> happy to see me when I get home.]
   - A. Kelly had to <u>act</u> quickly to avoid hitting the other car.
   - B. <u>Act</u> surprised even though you know about the party.
   - C. The first <u>act</u> of the play was funny.
   - D. Deon seemed sorry, but it was just an <u>act</u>.

2. [Sonya asked the waiter to <u>repeat</u> the daily specials.]
   - A. The TV show was a <u>repeat</u> of last week's episode.
   - B. <u>Repeat</u> customers get a discount.
   - C. The wallpaper should <u>repeat</u> the rose pattern in the sofa.
   - D. Will you <u>repeat</u> what you said a little louder?

3. [Lin installed a second <u>bar</u> in the closet.]
   - A. Sam hung a chin-up <u>bar</u> in the basement.
   - B. Marina stopped at the sandwich <u>bar</u> to order lunch.
   - C. The mayor wants to raise the <u>bar</u> for building new roads.
   - D. The police had to <u>bar</u> the crowd from going on the stage.

4. [Tap shoes have a metal <u>plate</u> on the toe or heel.]
   - A. Rico used a <u>plate</u> of glass to make a tabletop.
   - B. Set the <u>plate</u> of burgers on the counter.
   - C. Sal has a lot on his <u>plate</u> with his new job.
   - D. The jeweler plans to <u>plate</u> the ring in silver.

5. [The used car was in good <u>shape</u> even though it was ten years old.]
   - A. The square <u>shape</u> of those plates is interesting.
   - B. Arthur is worried about the <u>shape</u> of his finances.
   - C. It was difficult to <u>shape</u> the clay into a smooth bowl.
   - D. Staying calm will help you <u>shape</u> the outcome of the meeting.

6. [Look for a <u>sign</u> that points to Hartford.]
   - A. After you fill out the form, <u>sign</u> your name at the bottom.
   - B. The crossing guard held up one hand to make a <u>sign</u> for the traffic to stop.
   - C. A smile is a <u>sign</u> of happiness.
   - D. The park rules were printed on a <u>sign</u> near the entrance.

7. [There's a <u>note</u> on the door for the mail carrier.]

A. Be sure to <u>note</u> the changes in the schedule.

B. I can never hit the high <u>note</u> in that song.

C. <u>Note</u> your new address when you fill out the paperwork.

D. Sergio left a <u>note</u> saying he would be home soon.

8. [The fee is based on your <u>net</u> income.]

A. Sandy dipped her <u>net</u> into the lake and pulled out a fish.

B. Jamie's <u>net</u> pay was just enough to cover food and rent.

C. My daughter hopes to <u>net</u> the winning goal.

D. The volleyball barely made it over the <u>net</u>.

9. [Tomas bought a <u>pound</u> of tomatoes at the market.]

A. I lost one <u>pound</u> after running for a few days.

B. If you <u>pound</u> hard enough, someone will hear you.

C. Every pet we've had has been rescued from the <u>pound</u>.

D. I could feel my heart <u>pound</u> as I stood up to give my speech.

10. [Hector plans to <u>frame</u> the garden with roses.]

A. How do you plan to <u>frame</u> your argument?

B. The builder started on the house <u>frame</u>.

C. Daria wants to <u>frame</u> the photo and display it.

D. Yvonne is tall, but she has a small <u>frame</u>.

11. [Waiters should wear shoes that have good treads and won't <u>slip</u>.]

A. If the movie has started, <u>slip</u> into the theater quietly.

B. This pillow <u>slip</u> has a hole in it.

C. That idea may <u>slip</u> your mind if you don't write it down.

D. Be careful not to <u>slip</u> on the wet floor.

12. [There was a one-hour <u>wait</u> at the box office to buy tickets.]

A. Washing the dishes can <u>wait</u> until later.

B. The store hired two new clerks to <u>wait</u> on customers.

C. You may have a long <u>wait</u> to see the doctor.

D. The cars had to <u>wait</u> for the train to pass.

Check your answers on page 95.

GAIN
Learning Objective
*In this lesson, you
will learn to read
information on
a schedule.*

Schedules

A **schedule** shows **information** in a clear, easy-to-read **order**. It is usually organized by time or the order in which events take place. You may have read schedules to find movie times or the hours you work. The times, stops, and stations of buses and trains are always listed in a schedule.

Many schedules show information in a table. A **table** is made up of **rows and columns.** The organization of a table helps you find information quickly and easily. To find the subject of a schedule, first read its title and labels.

Grove Inc. Computer Training Schedule		
	Monday	Tuesday	Wednesday
Gina	9 A.M.–11 A.M.	1 P.M.–3 P.M.	2 P.M.–4 P.M.
Louise	10 A.M.–Noon	9 A.M.–11 A.M.	1 P.M.–3 P.M.
Darnel	2 P.M.–4 P.M.	9 A.M.–11 A.M.	10 A.M.–Noon

A **title** is usually at the top of a schedule. **Labels** may be used at the head of the columns and to the side of the rows.

To read the **rows** of a schedule, read across from left to right. To read the **columns,** read from top to bottom.

▶ Use both the column and the row to find information on a schedule. Follow these steps to find out when Gina is in training on Tuesday.

Find Gina's name. It is the label of the first row. Then find *Tuesday.* It is a column label. Read across the row from Gina's name to the *Tuesday* column. The block where the row and the column meet shows Gina's training time: 1 P.M.–3 P.M.

▶ Some schedules use a dash between items such as times or the ages of participants. The dash tells you to include all of the information between those two items. For example, the time of 1 P.M.–3 P.M. includes all of the time from 1:00 in the afternoon until 3:00 in the afternoon.

Understand It

1. Titles and labels help identify the information in a schedule.   **True**   **False**

2. To read a schedule, use both the rows and the columns.   **True**   **False**

Teacher Reminder
Review the teacher lesson at
www.mysteckvaughn.com/GAIN

Answers: True; True

Example

Look at the schedule on page 48. Who is in training from 10 A.M. to noon on Wednesday?

A. Louise

B. Darnel

C. Gina

D. Louise and Darnel

Step 1 ▶ Find the column in the schedule labeled *Wednesday.* Trace your finger down that column to find the time *10 A.M.–Noon.*

Step 2 ▶ Follow the row back to the labels on the left. Whose name is in that row? Darnel is training at that time.

Answer: B—Darnel

Think About It
Look for two pieces of information: the days of the week and the names of the participants.

Try It

Use the schedule below to answer the question that follows.

Decatur Township After-School and Day-Care Schedule		
Age of Child	Location	Days & Times
Ages 1–5 Ages 6–10	727 Rogers Ave.	Mon.–Sat., 6 A.M.–6 P.M.
Ages 7–14	1525 Laredo Dr.	Mon.–Fri., 3:30 P.M.–6 P.M.

Parents of a seven-year-old who need day care on Saturday from 9:00 A.M.–3:00 P.M. could take their child to

A. 1525 Laredo Dr.

B. 727 Rogers Ave.

C. either location.

D. neither location.

Your Answer: _____

Check Your Answer

In the days and times column, find the block that includes Saturday from 9:00 A.M.–3:00 P.M. Follow the row back to see if that time is available for a seven-year-old. Follow the row back again to find the location. Choose the correct answer.

Answer: The correct location is **727 Rogers Ave.**

Before You Begin
Read the title of the schedule and the labels of the columns.

TIPS & HINTS
Remember that a dash between items means to include everything between them. *Mon.–Fri.* means Monday, Tuesday, Wednesday, Thursday, and Friday.

Find the times when the parents need day care and find the age of the child.

CONNECTED LEARNING

LESSON **10**　BOOK **2**

GAIN Practice

Directions: Use the schedule below to answer the questions that follow.

Daytona Beach Shores Seasonal Tide Schedule* Sunglow Pier						
	Low Tide	**High Tide**	**Low Tide**	**High Tide**	**Sunrise**	**Sunset**
April 4	12:29 A.M.	6:50 A.M.	12:44 P.M.	6:50 P.M.	7:09 A.M.	7:44 P.M.
May 4	12:45 A.M.	7:10 A.M.	1:03 P.M.	7:10 P.M.	6:38 A.M.	8:02 P.M.
June 4	1:35 A.M.	8:04 A.M.	2:05 P.M.	8:26 P.M.	6:23 A.M.	8:21 P.M.
July 4	1:38 A.M.	8:00 A.M.	2:13 P.M.	8:38 P.M.	6:28 A.M.	8:28 P.M.
* Daylight Saving Time						

1. What time is low tide on the afternoon of May 4?

   A. 1:03 P.M.
   B. 12:45 A.M.
   C. 2:05 P.M.
   D. 2:13 P.M.

2. The earliest time the sun rises is on

   A. April 4.
   B. May 4.
   C. June 4.
   D. July 4.

3. The latest time the sun sets is on

   A. April 4.
   B. May 4.
   C. June 4.
   D. July 4.

4. What time is high tide on the evening of May 4?

   A. 7:10 A.M.
   B. 8:02 P.M.
   C. 7:10 P.M.
   D. 1:03 P.M.

5. On what day can you watch the sun set before 8:00 P.M.?

   A. April 4
   B. May 4
   C. June 4
   D. July 4

6. If you want to swim at low tide at the Fourth of July picnic, go in the water at

   A. 1:38 A.M.
   B. 12:44 P.M
   C. 8:38 P.M
   D. 2:13 P.M

Directions: Use the schedule below to answer the questions that follow.

Grove County Library July Schedule	
Mystery Book Club Join us to talk about the book *We'll Always Have Parrots* by Donna Andrews. Sign up by June 11th for a copy of the book.	Mondays & Wednesdays 10:00 A.M.–11:00 A.M.
Job and Career Counseling Help from experts on resumes, job searches, and filling out job applications. All ages.	Tuesdays 7:00 P.M.–8:00 P.M.
Grove County Blood Center Bloodmobile Come donate! Call the library or visit the GCBC Web site to sign up.	First Thursday of the month 2:00 P.M.–8:00 P.M.
Family Movie Night Enjoy watching a movie (to be announced). Free, with snacks and drinks provided.	Fridays 7:00 P.M.–9:00 P.M.
Your Home Workshop Trying to get organized? Learn about ways to get rid of clutter. A $5 fee includes organizers.	Saturdays 1:00 P.M.–2:00 P.M.

7. People who like to read will most likely participate in the

A. Mystery Book Club.
B. Job and Career Counseling.
C. Your Home Workshop.
D. Family Movie Night.

8. Which activity costs money?

A. Mystery Book Club
B. Family Movie Night
C. Grove County Bloodmobile
D. Your Home Workshop

9. When would you go to the library for information about looking for a job?

A. Tuesday at 7:00 P.M.
B. Saturday at 1:00 P.M.
C. Wednesday at 10:00 A.M.
D. Friday at 7:00 P.M.

10. If you wanted to learn more about organizing your closet, which activity would be the most helpful?

A. Mystery Book Club
B. Job and Career Counseling
C. Your Home Workshop
D. Family Movie Night

11. The Bloodmobile is at the library

A. once in the month.
B. once a week.
C. twice a week.
D. on weekends.

12. How many activities take place on the weekend?

A. one
B. two
C. three
D. four

Check your answers on page 96.

GAIN
Learning Objective
In this lesson, you will learn when to use capital letters.

Capitalization

Some words begin with a **capital letter**. Another word for capital letter is **uppercase letter**. Capital letters help make your writing clear. Here are some words that should be **capitalized**.

Capitalize the **first word in a sentence.**

> *The spare keys are under the doormat.*

Always capitalize the **pronoun** *I.*

> *Today I will get to work early.*

Capitalize proper nouns. A **proper noun** is the name of a specific person, place, or thing. Some examples of proper nouns include the names of streets (Cedar Lane), buildings (Empire State Building), sports arenas (Wrigley Field), parks (Central Park), and clubs or groups (Silver Gym).

> *Mac helped build a playground in Pine Park.*
> proper noun   proper noun

▶ A **common noun** is general. It names any person, place, animal, or thing. Do not capitalize common nouns.

> *We took our kids for a hike in the forest.*
>   common noun   common noun

Capitalize the first letter of a specific **city, state,** or **country.**

> *Jose lives in Ames, Iowa. He was born in Mexico.*
>   city   state   country

Capitalize a person's title. A person's **title** appears before his or her name. Do not capitalize common nouns that explain a title.

> *I met Dr. Alice Tamura, the principal of my son's school.*
>   title   name   common noun

Capitalize the names of **days** and **months.**

> *Cori began her new job on the last Monday in November.*
>   day   month

Understand It

1. A common noun is a specific person, place, or thing.   **True**   **False**

2. The name of a month begins with a capital letter.   **True**   **False**

Teacher Reminder
Review the teacher lesson at www.mysteckvaughn.com/GAIN

Answers: False; True

Example

Which sentence uses capital letters correctly?

A. The factory is closed in July and august.

B. In December, we will visit our parents in Miami.

C. We went with joe to buy a car in April.

D. My Birthday is in May.

Step 1 ▶ Read each sentence. Find the nouns. Which ones are proper nouns? Look for specific names, days, months, titles, and places. These should start with capital letters.

Step 2 ▶ Now look for common nouns. These are more general. They should not begin with capital letters. Choose the sentence that does not need to be corrected.

Answer: B—In December, we will visit our parents in Miami.

Think About It
Remember that common nouns should not be capitalized.

Try It

Choose the word that should be capitalized.

I called mayor Abban's office to ask about the town meeting.

A. mayor

B. office

C. meeting

D. town

Your Answer: _____

Check Your Answer

Read the sentence. Look at the words. The first word in a sentence should be capitalized. It is. The word *mayor* is a title. It comes before a person's name. Titles and names should be capitalized. The words *office, town,* and *meeting* are not proper nouns. They should not be capitalized.

Answer: The word that should be capitalized is **mayor.**

Before You Begin
Review the rules of capitalization. Apply each rule to the sentence.

Underline the nouns in the sentence. Then **circle** the proper nouns that should begin with a capital letter.

CONNECTED LEARNING

LESSON **1** \ LESSON **11** \ BOOK **15**

GAIN Practice

Directions: Choose the word that should be capitalized.

1. In august, I meet my cousins at a beach house.
   A. august
   B. house
   C. cousins
   D. beach

2. I brought mrs. Fuentes a can of gasoline to help start her car.
   A. mrs.
   B. can
   C. gasoline
   D. car

3. The rain in april hurt Lou's business.
   A. rain
   B. april
   C. hurt
   D. business

4. The flag at senator Sage's office ripped during the storm.
   A. flag
   B. senator
   C. storm
   D. office

5. The math class in the evening is taught by professor Julie Chang.
   A. class
   B. evening
   C. taught
   D. professor

6. Manny's new job is at a doctor's office in the small town of rugby.
   A. job
   B. doctor's
   C. town
   D. rugby

7. The pattis family has invited Ms. Leah Robb, a police officer, to dinner.
   A. pattis
   B. family
   C. dinner
   D. officer

8. I often take extra days off in the month of july.
   A. take
   B. days
   C. month
   D. july

9. When the ship came to town, we went to see our aunt, lieutenant Kay Drake.

A. ship
B. town
C. aunt
D. lieutenant

10. Petra read a story in the newspaper by governor J. K. Regis about solar energy.

A. story
B. newspaper
C. governor
D. energy

11. In january, Lee often makes extra money by shoveling snow.

A. january
B. money
C. shoveling
D. snow

12. None of the singers wanted to end the river tour and return to cleveland.

A. singers
B. wanted
C. tour
D. cleveland

13. Every morning, Mike follows nurse Keller's advice by walking to work.

A. morning
B. nurse
C. advice
D. work

14. My father was born in naples, Italy, 65 years ago.

A. father
B. born
C. naples
D. years

15. After I moved to florida, I got married and began a new business.

A. moved
B. florida
C. married
D. business

16. Yesterday, I read a poem about winds howling in march as the rainy season began.

A. poem
B. winds
C. march
D. season

Check your answers on page 97.

GAIN
Learning Objective
In this lesson, you will learn to use commas in a list.

Commas and Other Punctuation

In Lesson 6, you learned how to **end a sentence** with a period (.), a question mark (**?**), or an exclamation point (**!**).

.	for a statement or a command
?	for a question
!	for an exclamation

The **comma** is another type of **punctuation**. Commas separate sentence parts and items in a list. They help make the meaning of a sentence clear. Commas always go inside a sentence. Commas never appear at the end of a sentence.

Use commas to separate the names of **three or more items** in a list.

> *Serge put a shirt, tie, and jacket into the suitcase.*

The last two items in a list are always separated by either the word *and* or the word *or*.

> *Serge wore a shirt, tie, **and** jacket to the wedding.*

> *You may order a small, medium, **or** large drink.*

▶ Sometimes *and* is used to join two words to form one item. For example, in the sentence below, *macaroni and cheese* is one item in the list. Do not use a comma to separate the words.

> *My son ate <u>an apple</u>, <u>a sandwich</u>, and <u>macaroni **and** cheese</u>.*

If you add a comma after *macaroni,* it changes the list from three items to four items. It also changes what the boy ate. In the sentence below, the comma after *macaroni* makes *cheese* a separate item. In the first sentence, my son ate three things. In the sentence below, my son ate four things.

> *My son ate <u>an apple</u>, <u>a sandwich</u>, <u>macaroni</u>, and <u>cheese</u>.*

Understand It

1. Why do you use a comma to separate items in a list?

_____

2. Each item in a list can be a single word
or a group of words.   **True**   **False**

Teacher Reminder
Review the teacher lesson at www.mysteckvaughn.com/GAIN

Answers: to help make the meaning of the sentence clear; True

Example

Choose the correct punctuation.

The bank teller counted tens ＿＿ twenties, and fifties.

   A. .   **B. ,**   **C. !**   **D. ?**

Step 1 ▶ Read the sentence. Note that the missing punctuation mark is inside the sentence.

Step 2 ▶ The sentence lists three items: ten-dollar bills, twenty-dollar bills, and fifty-dollar bills. Choose the punctuation mark that separates items in a list.

Answer: B—(,)

Try It

Choose the correct punctuation.

1. Did Mr. or Mrs. Cook come to the wedding ＿＿

   A. .   **B. ,**   **C. !**   **D. ?**

Your Answer: ＿＿＿＿＿＿＿＿＿＿＿＿＿＿＿＿＿＿＿＿

Check Your Answer

The sentence is missing an end mark. The sentence asks a question.

Answer: The correct punctuation is (**?**).

2. Natalie, Terrel, Maria ＿＿ and Bridget decided to go back to school.

   A. .   **B. ,**   **C. !**   **D. ?**

Your Answer: ＿＿＿＿＿＿＿＿＿＿＿＿＿＿＿＿＿＿＿＿

Check Your Answer

The sentence lists four names. A punctuation mark that separates items in a list is needed between *Maria* and *Bridget*.

Answer: The correct punctuation is (**,**).

Think About It
Decide which answer choices are end punctuation marks.

Before You Begin
Review the rules for using punctuation marks in sentences.

TIPS & HINTS
Remember that commas separate three or more things in a list. End marks show that a sentence is a question, an exclamation, or a statement.

CONNECTED LEARNING

LESSON 6 ▷ LESSON 12 ▷ BOOK 2

GAIN Practice

Directions: Choose the correct punctuation.

1. Kima left the heavy ____ wet, and muddy boots outside.
   A. .
   B. ,
   C. !
   D. ?

2. Where is the post office ____
   A. .
   B. ,
   C. !
   D. ?

3. Tonight I must pay bills, walk the dog ____ and bake a cake.
   A. .
   B. ,
   C. !
   D. ?

4. Do you play chess ____
   A. .
   B. ,
   C. !
   D. ?

5. Myra reads, bikes ____ and sews for fun.
   A. .
   B. ,
   C. !
   D. ?

6. The new apartment needs a lamp ____ a stool, and a table.
   A. .
   B. ,
   C. !
   D. ?

7. This morning it was clear, sunny ____ and very cold outside.
   A. .
   B. ,
   C. !
   D. ?

8. Who hung a coat on the chair ____
   A. .
   B. ,
   C. !
   D. ?

9. Saul ____ Ginny, Reni, and Val hiked along the lake.

A. .
B. ,
C. !
D. ?

10. On Sunday I went to church ____ Magda went shopping, and Ben slept till noon.

A. .
B. ,
C. !
D. ?

11. I am so happy to see you ____

A. .
B. ,
C. !
D. ?

12. Please close the window ____

A. .
B. ,
C. !
D. ?

13. I drink soup, water ____ and tea when I am sick.

A. .
B. ,
C. !
D. ?

14. The stew has clams, shrimp, crabmeat ____ and cod.

A. .
B. ,
C. !
D. ?

15. Read the form and sign it at the bottom ____

A. .
B. ,
C. !
D. ?

16. I cannot remember if it was blue, purple ____ or green.

A. .
B. ,
C. !
D. ?

Check your answers on page 97.

GAIN
Learning Objective
In this lesson, you will learn to choose the correct verb form for the present tense.

Present Tense

Verbs can show **action**. Action verbs tell what the **subject** of a sentence **is doing.** In the sentence below, the verb *know* tells what the subject *she* is doing (knowing).

> <u>She</u> certainly <u>knows</u> this place.
> subject   verb

Linking verbs connect the subject with another word. These verbs show what the subject is, or is like. They do not show action.

> I <u>am</u> the owner.
> am tells who the subject *I* is (the owner)

> The flower <u>looks</u> pretty.
> looks tells what the subject *flower* is like (pretty)

If an action takes place now, use the **present tense** of the verb. Verbs change tense to show when an action takes place.

> I <u>want</u> a salad for lunch.
> want is happening now

Use the present tense to tell about **facts.**

> I <u>have</u> a car.   We <u>live</u> in South Port.
> fact about what I own   fact about where we live

Use the present tense to tell about actions that are **always true** or actions that **repeat.**

> Ocean water <u>tastes</u> salty.
> action is always true

> You <u>work</u> on Saturdays.
> action repeats

▶ Verbs can be regular or irregular. **Regular verbs** follow a pattern. For example, *want* is a regular verb. Its base form (*want*) does not change when the subject changes. Subjects can be singular or plural.

Regular Verb *Want*		
I (first-person singular)	**want**	a cup of coffee.
You (second-person singular or plural)	**want**	a cup of coffee.
He, She, It (third-person singular)	**wants**	a cup of coffee.
We (first-person plural)	**want**	a cup of coffee.
They (third-person plural)	**want**	a cup of coffee.

Notice that when the subject is *he, she,* or *it,* you add *-s* to the base form of a regular verb. Also use this verb form for subjects that name one person, animal, place, or thing.

> <u>Luis</u> <u>wants</u> to work the second shift today.
> one person

Understand It

1. Use the present tense of *want* in this sentence.

She _____ to go home.

2. The present tense is used to tell about things that are always true.   **True**   **False**

Answer: wants; True

Irregular verbs do not follow a pattern. The base word changes when the subject changes. Two important irregular verbs are **be** and **have**.

▶ The verb *be* has three forms in the present tense: *am, are,* and *is.* The present tense of *be* tells what is or what seems to be.

> The house <u>is</u> blue.
> present tense of *be*

The verb *have* has two forms in the present tense: *have* and *has.* The present tense of *have* tells what someone owns or holds.

> I <u>have</u> green eyes.
> present tense of *have*

The charts below shows the present tense forms of *be* and *have.*

Irregular Verb *Be*		
I	**am**	healthy.
You	**are**	healthy.
He, She, It	**is**	healthy.
We	**are**	healthy.
They	**are**	healthy.

Irregular Verb *Have*		
I	**have**	keys.
You	**have**	keys.
He, She, It	**has**	keys.
We	**have**	keys.
They	**have**	keys.

Example

Which form of the verb best completes the sentence?

Lucy and Dan ___?___ the daytime store managers.

   A. are   **B.** be   **C.** am   **D.** is

Step 1 ▶ Identify the missing verb. It is a form of the verb *be.*

Step 2 ▶ Identify the subject of the sentence. The subject names two people, *Lucy and Dan.* The plural subject takes a plural verb. Choose the form of the verb that goes with the subject *they.*

Answer: A—are

Think About It

Remember that the verb *be* has three forms in the present tense: *am, are,* and *is.* Decide which form agrees with the subject.

CONNECTED LEARNING

Try It

Choose the verb form that best completes the sentence.

1. We __?__ to meet the Coopers at the lake today.

    A. wants

    B. has wanted

    C. want

    D. be wanting

Your Answer: _____

Check Your Answer

Find the subject of the sentence. Ask yourself, "Who is doing the action?" *We* is the subject of the sentence. *We* names more than one person. It is a first-person plural subject. A first-person plural subject takes the plural form of the regular verb *want*. The plural form of *want* is *want*.

Answer: The correct verb form is **want.**

2. He __?__ the person who repairs our computer.

    A. are

    B. be

    C. am

    D. is

Your Answer: _____

Check Your Answer

This sentence does not show action. The verb is a form of *be.* Recall that *be* has three forms in the present tense: *am, is,* and *are.* The verb must agree with the subject. Find the subject of the sentence. Ask yourself, "Who is the sentence about?" *He* is the subject of the sentence. *He* is a third-person singular subject. The verb *is* links *He* with *the person who repairs our computer.* The verb *is* agrees in person and number with the subject *He.*

Answer: The correct verb form is **is.**

GAIN Practice

Directions: Choose the verb form that best completes the sentence.

1. We __?__ fish once a week.

   A. cooks
   B. cooking
   C. cook
   D. was cooked

2. Rafael __?__ to relax after work today.

   A. wants
   B. have wanted
   C. want
   D. be wanting

3. Bob and Terry __?__ to the radio.

   A. listens
   B. was listening
   C. listen
   D. has listened

4. Lois __?__ our best customer.

   A. are
   B. be
   C. am
   D. is

5. I __?__ never late for work.

   A. are
   B. be
   C. am
   D. is

6. We sometimes __?__ to walk in the rain.

   A. likes
   B. like
   C. has liked
   D. was liking

Continued on next page ▶

GAIN Practice *continued*

7. You __?__ a dentist's appointment today.
   A. has
   B. have
   C. was having
   D. having

8. Aska __?__ the trumpet in a band.
   A. playing
   B. has playing
   C. play
   D. plays

9. I __?__ food for McGuire's restaurant.
   A. deliver
   B. delivers
   C. were delivering
   D. has delivered

10. Where __?__ you?
    A. are
    B. be
    C. am
    D. is

11. Who __?__ salad for lunch?
    A. eaten
    B. eat
    C. eats
    D. eating

12. The kids __?__ a puppy!
    A. has
    B. have
    C. were having
    D. having

13. The librarian usually __?__ me find good books.
    A. help
    B. helping
    C. were helping
    D. helps

14. They all __?__ to read the newspaper every evening.
    A. want
    B. has wanted
    C. be wanting
    D. wants

15. Where __?__ your home?

   A. be
   B. are
   C. is
   D. am

16. The neighbors __?__ their car every morning.

   A. moves
   B. move
   C. was moving
   D. moving

17. I __?__ to take a vacation.

   A. want
   B. wants
   C. wanting
   D. were wanting

18. We __?__ happy to hear that your baby is healthy.

   A. is
   B. am
   C. are
   D. be

19. My car __?__ 100,000 miles on it.

   A. having
   B. have
   C. were having
   D. has

20. Chi __?__ babysitters for us.

   A. finding
   B. finds
   C. were finding
   D. find

21. The film __?__ sadly.

   A. end
   B. ending
   C. were ending
   D. ends

22. Hakan __?__ that his bank closes at 3 P.M. on Saturdays.

   A. were knowing
   B. knows
   C. knowing
   D. know

Check your answers on page 98.

GAIN
Learning Objective
In this lesson, you will learn to choose the correct past tense and future tense verb form.

Past and Future Tenses

In Lesson 13, you learned about the present tense of verbs. Remember that a verb's **tense** shows **when the action takes place.** Verbs can be in the present tense, past tense, or future tense.

The **past tense** tells about **completed actions.** These are actions that took place in the past. To form the past tense of a **regular verb,** add *-ed* to the end of the verb.

> *I* <u>walk</u> *to work.*
> present tense

> *I* <u>walked</u> *to work.*
> past tense

Irregular verbs form the past tense by changing their spelling.

Present and Past Tenses of Irregular Verbs			
Present	**Past**	**Present**	**Past**
catch	caught	see	saw
choose	chose	sing	sang
drive	drove	sit	sat
eat	ate	speak	spoke
fall	fell	swim	swam
grow	grew	swing	swung
hear	heard	take	took
ring	rang	tell	told
rise	rose	think	thought
run	ran	write	wrote

▶ The past tense of a regular or irregular verb is the same for every subject. For example, *lost* is the past tense of *lose.*

> Singular: **I** <u>lost</u> my pen. **You** <u>lost</u> your pen. **She** <u>lost</u> her pen.

> Plural: **We** <u>lost</u> our pens. **You** <u>lost</u> your pens. **They** <u>lost</u> their pens.

The **future tense** describes something that **has not yet happened.** It is formed with the **helping verb *will*,** plus the **base form of the verb.**

> *On Monday, Derek* <u>will move</u> *to another department.*
> helping verb *(will)* + base verb *(move)*

The base form of *be* is *be.* The base form of *have* is *have.*

> *Tanisha* <u>will be</u> *late for work. She* <u>will have</u> *to explain this to her boss.*

Teacher Reminder
Review the teacher lesson at
www.mysteckvaughn.com/GAIN

Understand It

1. How do regular verbs show the past tense?

_____

2. To form the future tense, use the helping verb
will with the base form of the verb.   **True**   **False**

Answers: add -*ed* to the end of the verb; True

Example

Which verb form best completes the sentence?

No one ___?___ the thief until he tripped.

A. hears   **B.** hear   **C.** heard   **D.** will hear

Step 1 ▶ Read the sentence. Find words that show if the action is in the past, present, or future. The verb *tripped* is in the past tense. It tells you that the thief acted in the past.

Step 2 ▶ Choose a past tense verb to complete the sentence. The answer choices are all forms of the verb *hear*. *Hear* is an irregular verb. You form the past tense of *hear* by changing the spelling. Choose the past tense form of the irregular verb *hear*.

Answer: C—heard

Example

Which verb form best completes the sentence?

Bret ___?___ the floor early next Friday morning.

A. washed

C. was washing

B. will wash

D. will washing

Step 1 ▶ Read the sentence. Is the action in the past, present, or future? The words *next Friday morning* place the action in the future.

Step 2 ▶ Use the future tense of *wash* to complete the sentence. Remember that you form the future tense by using the helping verb *will* with the base form of the verb.

Answer: B—will wash

Think About It
Irregular verbs change their spelling to show the past tense.

Think About It
Look for clues in the sentence that tell you if the action is in the past, present, or future.

CONNECTED LEARNING

LESSON **13** > LESSON **14** > LESSON **15**

Before You Begin

Underline words that help you decide whether the action takes place in the past, present, or future.

TIPS & HINTS

Remember that irregular verbs show the past tense by changing their spelling.

Remember that a future tense verb is formed by placing *will* in front of the base form of the verb.

Write the tense of each verb form next to the answer choices.

Try It

Choose the verb form that best completes the sentence.

1. Gregor ___?___ his boss to work yesterday.

   A. driven

   B. is driving

   C. drives

   D. drove

Your Answer: _____

Check Your Answer

Decide if the action takes place in the past, present, or future. The word *yesterday* places the action in the past. The sentence is telling you that Gregor did something yesterday. Use the past tense of the irregular verb *drive*.

Answer: The correct verb form is **drove.**

2. Hector and Jerome ___?___ next week's basketball game.

   A. watched

   B. will watch

   C. watches

   D. have watched

Your Answer: _____

Check Your Answer

Find words that tell you when the action takes place. The words *next week's basketball game* tell you that the sentence is about a future action. Hector and Jerome's action has not happened yet. Use the helping verb *will* to form the future tense of the verb *watch*.

Answer: The correct verb form is **will watch.**

GAIN Practice

Directions: Choose the verb form that best completes the sentence.

1. They __?__ beans and peppers in their garden.

   A. grew
   B. grows
   C. growing
   D. has grown

2. I __?__ my sister's family on Sunday.

   A. seen
   B. will see
   C. is seeing
   D. were seeing

3. Andrei __?__ drove my car to the service station.

   A. are driving
   B. drived
   C. drove
   D. were driving

4. We __?__ to stay at home for the holiday.

   A. chosen
   B. chose
   C. choosing
   D. is choosing

5. We __?__ pictures of the sunset.

   A. taked
   B. taken
   C. took
   D. was taking

6. Rebecca __?__ in her rocking chair.

   A. sit
   B. sitted
   C. will sat
   D. sat

7. I __?__ a bass on our fishing trip.

   A. catched
   B. caught
   C. will caught
   D. catching

8. Samuel __?__ across the lake.

   A. am swimming
   B. swim
   C. will swim
   D. swimmed

Continued on next page ▶

GAIN Practice *continued*

9. The sun ___?___ over the mountains.
   A. rise
   B. will rising
   C. rose
   D. were rising

10. Gerard ___?___ his hat at the stadium.
    A. has lose
    B. losed
    C. losing
    D. lost

11. I ___?___ about taking a cooking class.
    A. thought
    B. will thinking
    C. thinks
    D. has thought

12. Chet ___?___ me about his son's new home.
    A. tell
    B. have telling
    C. will telling
    D. told

13. Jim ___?___ about Calla and Ron's wedding plans.
    A. heard
    B. heared
    C. hear
    D. hearing

14. Miguel ___?___ his car at the car wash.
    A. wash
    B. will wash
    C. have washed
    D. washing

15. I ___?___ to her about moving to the city.
    A. speaking
    B. speaks
    C. spoke
    D. spoken

16. A rabbit ___?___ the lettuce I planted.
    A. ate
    B. eaten
    C. have eaten
    D. eating

17. Mitch __?__ his son waving a banner at the game.

A. seen
B. seeing
C. saw
D. have saw

18. Sherise __?__ her neighbor's doorbell twice.

A. rang
B. ringing
C. ring
D. ringed

19. I __?__ this bell to hear how it sounds.

A. ringing
B. be ringing
C. will ring
D. is ringing

20. Ruben __?__ his dance partner.

A. swing
B. swung
C. swinging
D. were swinging

21. Sui Ky __?__ a story for her children.

A. am writing
B. has wrote
C. wrote
D. writing

22. Megan __?__ a song to her three sleepy nieces.

A. sang
B. sing
C. singing
D. am singing

23. I __?__ on the icy sidewalk again.

A. falls
B. fell
C. were falling
D. is falling

24. Jacee __?__ five miles in Sunday's race.

A. runned
B. have run
C. run
D. will run

Check your answers on page 100.

GAIN
Learning Objective
In this lesson, you will learn to find and correct errors in subject-verb agreement, verb tense, and capitalization.

Proofreading

When you proofread, you look for ways to improve your writing. **Proofreading** is reading to find and correct errors.

One common error writers make is in **subject-verb agreement.** You know that the **subject** of a sentence is the person or thing doing the action. The **verb** must agree with the subject in **person** and **number.** The chart below shows subject-verb agreement for the verb *cook* in the present tense.

Person	Singular	Plural
First (*I, we*)	I **cook**	we **cook**
Second (*you, you*)	you **cook**	you **cook**
Third (*he, she, it, they*)	he/she/it **cooks**	they **cook**

A subject can be in the first, second, or third person. The subject's number can be singular (one) or plural (more than one). Do not let words that separate a subject and a verb confuse you.

*The <u>pot</u> of beans **cooks** on the stove.*
singular subject   singular verb

For **regular verbs,** the letter *-s* is added to the present tense verb when the subject is third-person singular.

Jonathan <u>cooks</u> vegetables on the campfire.

▶ Some regular verbs end in *-o, -s, -ch,* or *-sh.* To form the present tense of those verbs, add *-es* when the subject is third-person singular.

Chloe <u>washes</u> her clothes with a scent-free soap.
present tense, third-person singular *(wash + -es)*

Some regular verbs end in *-y.* Replace the *-y* with the letters *-ies* to form a present tense, third-person singular verb.

Mayda <u>studies</u> for a nursing test.

You know that **irregular verbs** change spelling to show tense. Irregular verbs also change spelling to agree with their subjects.

Person	Singular	Plural
First (*I, we*)	I **am**	we **are**
Second (*you, you*)	you **are**	you **are**
Third (*he, she, it, they*)	he/she/it **is**	they **are**

Teacher Reminder
Review the teacher lesson at www.mysteckvaughn.com/GAIN

Understand It

1. Write the verb *move* for first-, second-, and third-person singular subjects.

_____

2. Plural subjects in a sentence need singular verbs.   **True**   **False**

Answers: I move, you move, he/she/it moves; False

As you proofread, make sure the verb tenses are correct. Most of the time, you want to use the same verb tenses throughout the sentence or paragraph.

> I <u>ate</u> an apple, <u>washed</u> the dishes, and <u>went</u> out.
> past tense   past tense   past tense

► Sometimes actions happen at different times. Change the verb tenses to show different times. Use the present tense to tell about the future after *if*, *when*, *before*, *as soon as*, *after*, and other **time words**.

> I <u>am</u> sure that Alyssa <u>will wash</u> the car tomorrow **after** I <u>leave</u>.
> present tense   future tense   present tense

Look for **capitalization** errors in your writing. Remember to capitalize the first letter of **proper nouns**. Common nouns are not capitalized.

> I drove through eight <u>states</u> from <u>Detroit, Michigan</u>, to <u>Austin, Texas</u>.
> common noun   city, state   city, state

Example

In which sentence is the verb form incorrect?

  A. The head lineman in my crew tells too many jokes.

  B. It is illegal to sell elephant ivory.

  C. A book about home repairs are on the table.

  D. We are on vacation this week.

Step 1 ► Read the sentences. Identify the subject and main verb in each sentence.

Step 2 ► Decide if the subjects and verbs agree in person and number.

Answer: C—A book about home repairs are on the table.

Think About It
Look for the subject. The verb must agree with the subject, not words that may appear between them.

Circle the subjects and verbs in the sentences. Draw a line to connect each verb with its subject.

TIPS & HINTS

Remember that when the subject is *he, she,* or *it,* you add *-s* to the present tense form of a regular verb.

Notice which nouns are common and which are proper. Proper nouns begin with a capital letter.

Try It

Choose the <u>underlined</u> section that has an error in it. If there are no errors, choose D.

1. Rocky <u>will drive</u> me <u>to Miami</u> after <u>he clean</u> his car. <u>No error</u>.

               A.   B.   C.   D.

Your Answer: _____

Check Your Answer

Read the sentence. Check that the two proper nouns begin with a capital letter. Check that subjects and verbs agree. Look at section C. The word *he* is the subject of the verb *clean*. *He* is a third-person singular subject. The correct verb form of *clean* with a third-person singular subject is *cleans*.

Answer: The section that has an error in it is **he clean.**

2. I <u>will find</u> a new job <u>when we is back</u> from <u>Boston</u>. <u>No error</u>.

             A.   B.   C.   D.

Your Answer: _____

Check Your Answer

Read the sentence. Check to make sure that subjects and verbs agree. Make sure that any proper nouns begin with a capital letter. Now reread section B. The subject is the first-person plural *we*. The verb *is* does not agree with this subject. The first-person plural form of *be* is *are*, not *is*. The subject and verb do not agree.

Answer: The section that has an error in it is **when we is back.**

GAIN Practice

Directions: Choose the underlined section that has an error in it. If there are no errors, choose D.

1. <u>I worked</u> at a school <u>in chicago</u> one day a week before <u>I started</u> my new job. <u>No error</u>.
       A.   B.   C.   D.

2. Now <u>I work</u> five days a week at <u>Waverly Gardens</u> in <u>Smithtown</u>. <u>No error</u>.
         A.   B.   C.   D.

3. Every day, <u>Ted and I washes</u> the glass walls of the <u>indoor garden</u> before <u>we go</u>. <u>No error</u>.
               A.   B.   C.   D.

4. <u>I is liking</u> <u>to take my kids</u> to the butterfly garden <u>to watch new butterflies fly</u>. <u>No error</u>.
       A.   B.   C.   D.

5. <u>I water</u> the flowers and <u>pulls out the weeds</u> as <u>I work in the gardens</u>. <u>No error</u>.
       A.   B.   C.   D.

6. <u>Many people will be</u> at <u>the gardens</u> when <u>Mr. Abdul talk</u> about insects. <u>No error</u>.
         A.   B.   C.   D.

Continued on next page ▶

7. Ladybugs are helpful because they eat bugs that harms the flowers. No error.

          A.   B.   C.   D.

8. Next week, Mr. Abdul will discuss how hoverflies is good for gardens. No error.

          A.   B.   C.   D.

9. I will visit the Texas Discovery Gardens when we are in dallas on vacation. No error.

          A.   B.   C.   D.

10. I will take a class on organic gardening when I are at the gardens in Texas. No error.

          A.   B.   C.   D.

11. My family is happy that I begin my new job and learned about plants and gardens. No error.

          A.   B.   C.   D.

12. We move to the city in August of last year before the baby was born. No error.

          A.   B.   C.   D.

13. My brother-in-law took my sons to a park and practice soccer drills with them. No error.
          A.   B.   C.   D.

14. The stack of invoices sit on the table where Kyra found it. No error.
          A.   B.   C.   D.

15. Where will you eat dinner when you met your wife after you leave work today? No error.
          A.   B.   C.   D.

16. My wife said that I worry too much after I are telling her that Lou lost his job. No error.
        A.   B.   C.   D.

17. The pile of dirty clothes are in the basket, the soap is on the table, and I am ready to go.
              A.   B.   C.

No error.
    D.

18. Next month, I surprised my husband when I get a dog for him on his birthday. No error.
                   A.   B.   C.   D.

Check your answers on page 100.

Congratulations!

You've completed the last nine lessons of *GAIN Essentials* English Skills Book 1.
In this section of the book, you worked through the GAIN Review Topics below.
Place a checkmark next to the Review Topics that you think you have mastered:

- ☐ Understand eight-word sentences.

- ☐ Identify the missing word in a sentence.

- ☐ Understand meanings of words with multiple meanings.

- ☐ Retrieve information from a schedule.

- ☐ Capitalize the names of months and cities.

- ☐ Capitalize the title preceding a personal name.

- ☐ Use commas in a list.

- ☐ Choose the correct verb form of a regular verb in the present tense.

- ☐ Choose the correct verb form of an irregular verb in the present tense.

- ☐ Choose the correct verb form of an irregular verb in the past tense and the future tense.

- ☐ Find and correct grammatical errors: regular and irregular verbs, future tense, subject-verb agreement, capitalization.

Check Your Progress

Now it's time to check your progress. The items on pages 79–83 of the *GAIN Check In 2* allow you to self-check your mastery of the concepts. Unlike the actual GAIN, the *Check In* is not timed, so take your time. Read each item carefully and choose the correct answer.

Directions: Choose the best answer.

1. { Destiny parked her car near the grocery store. }

   Who parked it?

   A. Destiny
   B. car
   C. grocery
   D. store

2. { Carl stores his gas grill in the garage. }

   What does he store?

   A. Carl
   B. gas
   C. grill
   D. garage

Directions: Choose the word that best completes the sentence.

3. Seth works only part-time, so he ___?___ about spending $90 for a concert ticket.

   A. inquired
   B. insisted
   C. hesitated
   D. celebrated

4. Juanita was ___?___ when the teacher didn't return her call.

   A. relieved
   B. satisfied
   C. pleased
   D. offended

Directions: Determine the meaning of the <u>underlined</u> word in the sentence in brackets. Then choose the answer in which that word has the same meaning.

5. [Roman had to <u>lean</u> against the door because he felt dizzy.]

   A. Don't <u>lean</u> against that freshly painted wall.
   B. You can <u>lean</u> on me if you need help.
   C. I <u>lean</u> toward the candidate who supports public schools.
   D. Many runners have a <u>lean</u> build.

6. [Snakes <u>shed</u> their skin as they grow.]

   A. The rakes and shovels are stored in the tool <u>shed</u>.
   B. Some breeds of dogs <u>shed</u> more than others.
   C. His message of peace <u>shed</u> hope on the community.
   D. He <u>shed</u> some tears from pure relief.

Continued on next page ▶

Directions: Use the schedule below to answer the questions that follow.

Community Center Summer Schedule*		
Activity	**Monday–Friday**	**Saturday**
Step Aerobics	Mon., Wed., Fri. 7 A.M.–8 A.M. Tue., Thurs. 9 A.M.–10 A.M.	
Basketball	Adult Leagues Mon., Wed., Fri. 6 P.M.–10 P.M.	
	Youth Leagues Tue., Thurs. 2 P.M.–5 P.M.	
First Aid/CPR (Note: classes held in the gym's conference room.)		9 A.M.–5 P.M.
Volleyball	Adult Leagues Tue., Thurs. 6 P.M.–10 P.M.	Youth Leagues 9 A.M.–Noon
Yoga	Mon., Wed., Fri. 9 A.M.–10 A.M. Tue., Thurs. 7 A.M.–8 A.M.	
Open Gym		Noon–4 P.M.

* This is a schedule for the gymnasium. Please see the front office bulletin board for the complete summer schedule of activities and meeting rooms.

7. What time are Step Aerobics classes held on Wednesday?

    A. 7 A.M.–8 A.M.
    B. 6 P.M.–10 P.M.
    C. 9 A.M.–10 A.M.
    D. 9 A.M.–Noon

8. On which day does the gym have open time?

    A. Monday
    B. Tuesday
    C. Friday
    D. Saturday

9. Where can you find the schedule for outdoor activities?

    A. in the gym's conference room
    B. on the outdoor fields
    C. on the front office bulletin board
    D. in the gymnasium

10. When do the youth basketball leagues play?

    A. Tue., Thurs. 9 A.M.–10 A.M.
    B. Mon., Wed., Fri. 6 P.M.–10 P.M.
    C. Sat. 9 A.M.–Noon
    D. Tue., Thurs. 2 P.M.–5 P.M.

11. Des will see mayor Angus in his office at two o'clock this afternoon.

    A. see
    B. mayor
    C. office
    D. afternoon

14. In the evening, we watched bats _____ swallows, and swifts fly by us.

    A. .
    B. ,
    C. !
    D. ?

12. In february, we take our girls sledding at a park with a hill.

    A. february
    B. girls
    C. park
    D. hill

15. When will you arrive in Los Gatos _____

    A. .
    B. ,
    C. !
    D. ?

13. If you like good jazz and spicy food, go to New orleans.

    A. jazz
    B. food
    C. go
    D. orleans

16. Callie, Alex, Viv _____ and Walt went dancing.

    A. .
    B. ,
    C. !
    D. ?

Continued on next page ▶

GAIN Check In *continued*

Directions: Choose the verb form that best completes the sentence.

17. I __?__ first base on the men's team.

    A. is playing

    B. has played

    C. play

    D. plays

18. Fiona __?__ a catcher on the women's team.

    A. are

    B. were

    C. am

    D. is

19. Last week, Shin __?__ a new sign for the store.

    A. buys

    B. bought

    C. be buying

    D. have bought

20. Last night, the picnic basket __?__ under the tree.

    A. were

    B. are

    C. was

    D. be

21. Ang __?__ the truck tire in the morning.

    A. change

    B. will change

    C. changing

    D. have changed

22. We __?__ the best carpenters.

    A. am

    B. is

    C. has been

    D. are

Directions: Choose the underlined section that has an error in it.
If there are no errors, choose D.

23. We will watch the children when you is ready to walk to Mrs. Lang's house. No error.
    A.   B.   C.   D.

24. Lourdes carry the baby inside and puts her in the crib to take a nap. No error.
    A.   B.   C.   D.

25. Mr. Ides gave us tickets to see the game at the stadium in newark. No error.
    A.   B.   C.   D.

26. I will visit Remy after he returns from his trip to buy metal art in Haiti. No error.
    A.   B.   C.   D.

27. A vase of flowers sit on the same table that has three apples on it. No error.
    A.   B.   C.   D.

28. Next, you will learn that the eyes of a starfish is on the ends of its arms. No error.
    A.   B.   C.   D.

Check Your Answers

Now that you've completed *GAIN Check In 2*, check your answers on page 101.
Then complete the *Performance Assessment Chart* on page 89. This will help you
determine whether you need to review any lessons or are ready to take the Online
Posttest Assessment. Did you master all the concepts you checked on page 78?

Link to Online Posttest Assessment

Congratulations!

You've completed *GAIN Essentials* English Skills Book 1! You've worked through the GAIN Review Topics for Educational Functioning Levels 1 and 2.

Now you're ready to take the Online Posttest Assessment. This test will allow you to demonstrate your understanding of the concepts from *GAIN Essentials* English Skills Book 1.

Please go to
www.mysteckvaughn.com/GAIN
to take the Online
Posttest Assessment.

GAIN Essentials English Skills Book 2

After you complete the Online Posttest Assessment for *GAIN Essentials* English Skills Book 1, you are ready to study *GAIN Essentials* English Skills Book 2.

GAIN Essentials English Skills Book 2 addresses the GAIN Review Topics at Educational Functioning Levels 3 and 4. In that book, you will complete lessons that teach you to:

- Choose the correct form of a verb in the present tense

- Choose the correct form of an irregular verb in the present tense

- Choose the correct verb form in a sentence with an *if* clause

- Order phrases logically using language clues

- Identify a complete sentence

- Identify well-constructed sentences with effective prepositional and other phrases

- Find and correct grammatical errors

- Identify the missing word in a sentence

- Determine the meaning of a word from context

- Understand the meanings of words with multiple meanings

- Retrieve information from step-by-step directions

- Understand and retrieve information from a reference article

- Understand and retrieve information in simple prose

- Select the correct adverb in a sentence

- Choose the appropriate preposition

- Select the correct pronoun form

- Distinguish between facts and opinions in simple prose

- Retrieve information from a schedule

Performance Assessment Chart

GAIN Check In 1 (Lessons 1–6)

The following chart can help you determine your strengths and weaknesses with the GAIN Review Topics listed below. You must master the GAIN Review Topics to perform well on the *GAIN Test of English Skills*.

Complete *GAIN Check In 1* on pages 28–33. Then check your answers using pages 93 and 94 of the *Answers and Explanations* at the back of the book.

On the chart below:

- Circle the question numbers that you answered incorrectly.

- Reference the lesson page numbers for the questions you circled. Review these pages to be sure you understand the GAIN Review Topic before moving to the next section.

Question Numbers	GAIN Review Topics for Lessons 1–6	Lesson Page Numbers
1, 2, 3, 4, 5, 6	**Alphabet:** Choose the uppercase letter in a five-letter sequence	4–7
7, 8, 9, 10, 11	**Word Recognition:** Match pictures to words	8–11
24, 25, 26	**Information Retrieval:** Identify the parts of a complete mailing address and phone number	12–15
18, 19, 20, 21, 22, 23	**Words in Context:** Identify the missing word in a sentence	16–19
12, 13, 14, 15, 16, 17	**Reading Comprehension:** Understand eight-word sentences	20–23
27, 28, 29	**Punctuation:** Use a question mark, a period, and an exclamation point	24–27

GAIN Check In 2 (Lessons 7–15)

The following chart can help you determine your strengths and weaknesses with the GAIN Review Topics listed below. You must master the GAIN Review Topics to perform well on the *GAIN Test of English Skills*.

Complete *GAIN Check In 2* on pages 78–83. Then check your answers using pages 101 and 102 of the *Answers and Explanations* at the back of the book.

On the chart below:

- Circle the question numbers that you answered incorrectly.

- Reference the lesson page numbers for the questions you circled. Review these pages to be sure you understand the GAIN Review Topic before taking the Online Posttest Assessment.

Question Numbers	GAIN Review Topics for Lessons 7–15	Lesson Page Numbers
1, 2	**Reading Comprehension:** Understand eight-word sentences	36–39
3, 4	**Words in Context:** Identify the missing word in a sentence	40–43
5, 6	**Words in Context:** Understand the meanings of words with multiple meanings	44–47
7, 8, 9, 10	**Charts:** Retrieve information from a schedule	48–51
12	**Capitalization:** Capitalize the names of months and cities	52–55
11, 13	**Capitalization:** Capitalize the title preceding a personal name	52–55
14, 15, 16	**Punctuation:** Use commas in a list and use other punctuation	56–59
17	**Verb Forms:** Choose the correct form of a regular verb in the present tense	60–65
18, 22	**Verb Forms:** Choose the correct form of an irregular verb in the present tense	60–65
19, 20	**Verb Forms:** Choose the correct form of an irregular verb in the past tense and the future tense	66–71
23, 24, 25, 26, 27, 28	**Proofreading:** Find and correct grammatical errors	72–77

Answers and Explanations

Lesson 1 (pages 6–7)

1. C. G
Option C is correct. *G* is the letter that comes between *F* and *H*. Option A is incorrect becausè *E* comes before these letters. Options B and D are incorrect because *K* and *L* come after these letters.

2. D. X
Option D is correct. *X* is the letter that comes between *W* and *Y*. Options A and C are incorrect because *U* and *T* come before these letters. Option B is incorrect because *A* is at the beginning of the alphabet, not the end.

3. A. O
Option A is correct. *O* is the letter that comes between *N* and *P*. Options B and D are incorrect because *Q* and *R* come right after these letters. Option C is incorrect because *K* comes before these letters.

4. B. B
Option B is correct. *B* is the letter that comes right before *C*. Options A and C are incorrect because *G* and *L* come after these letters. Option D is incorrect because *A* comes right before *B*, not *C*.

5. D. N
Option D is correct. *N* is the letter that comes right after the letter *M*. Option A is incorrect because *I* comes before *J*. Options B and C are incorrect because neither *P* nor *O* comes right after *M*.

6. C. R
Option C is correct. The letter *R* comes between *Q* and *S*. Option A is incorrect because *T* comes after these letters. Options B and D are incorrect because *M* and *L* come before these letters.

7. C. T
Option C is correct. The letter *T* comes between *S* and *U*. Options A and D are incorrect because *X* and *Z* come after these letters. Option B is incorrect because *Q* comes before these letters.

8. D. O
Option D is correct. *O* is the letter that comes between *N* and *P*. Option A is incorrect because *M* comes before these letters. Options B and C are incorrect because *S* and *T* come after these letters.

9. B. H
Option B is correct. *H* is the letter that comes right before *I*. Options A and D are incorrect because *G* and *F* come before *H*, not right before *I*. Option C is incorrect because *M* comes after these letters.

10. A. U
Option A is correct. The letter *U* comes between *T* and *V*. Option B is incorrect because *Q* comes before these letters. Options C and D are incorrect because *W* and *Y* come after these letters.

11. D. G
Option D is correct. The letter *G* comes after *F* and before *H* in the alphabet. Option A is incorrect because *D* comes before these letters. Options B and C are incorrect because *K* and *J* come after these letters.

12. B. L
Option B is correct. The letter *L* comes right after *K* in the alphabet. Options A and D are incorrect because *G* and *E* come before these letters. Option C is incorrect because *M* comes after *L*, not right after *K*.

13. C. W
Option C is correct. The letter *W* comes between *V* and *X*. Options A, B, and D are incorrect because *Q, U,* and *T* come before these letters.

14. B. D
Option B is correct. The letter *D* comes after *C* and before *E*. Options A and C are incorrect because *G* and *H* come after these letters. Option D is incorrect because *A* comes before these letters.

15. A. J
Option A is correct. The letter *J* comes after *I* and before *K*. Options B and C are incorrect because *C* and *F* come before these letters. Option D is incorrect because *L* comes after these letters.

16. D. Q
Option D is correct. The letter *Q* comes between *P* and *R*. Options A and C are incorrect because *N* and *O* both come before these letters. Option B is incorrect because *U* comes after these letters.

Lesson 2 (pages 10–11)

1. C. pen
Option C is correct. The picture shows a pen. Option A is incorrect because it does not have the right middle sound. Option B is incorrect because it does not have the right beginning sound. Option D is incorrect because it does not have the right middle or ending sound.

2. A. train
Option A is correct. The picture shows a train. Option B is incorrect because it does not have the correct middle or ending sound. Option C is incorrect because it does not have the correct middle or ending sound. Option D is incorrect because it does not have the correct middle or ending sound. *Track* is related to *train*, but it does not match the picture.

3. A. star
Option A is correct. The picture shows a star. Option B is incorrect because it does not begin or end with the correct letter sound. Only the *ar* sound is the same. Option C is incorrect because it has a different middle and ending sound. Option D is incorrect because it has a different middle and ending sound.

4. C. button
Option C is correct. The picture shows a button. Option A is incorrect because it does not begin with a *b*. Option B is incorrect because a button is part of a jacket. The two are related, but *jacket* has different letter sounds. Option D is incorrect because it does not have the correct ending sound.

5. C. ear
Option C is correct. The picture shows an ear. Option A is incorrect because the sound of *m is* not the right ending sound. Option B is incorrect because the letters of *eye* make one sound, which does not match any sound in *ear*. Option D is incorrect because it has a different beginning sound than the picture name.

6. D. bell
Option D is correct. The picture shows a bell. Option A is incorrect because *belt* has a *t* sound at the end. This does not match *bell*. Option B is incorrect because it does not have the correct middle or ending sound. Option C is incorrect because it does not have the correct middle sound.

7. C. picture of a chicken
Option C is correct. The word is *chicken*. Option A is incorrect because a feather is only a part of a chicken. Option B is incorrect because the middle and ending sounds of *chair* are different from those of *chicken*. Option D is incorrect because *chicken* and *children* have different middle sounds.

8. C. spoon
Option C is correct. The picture shows a spoon. Option A is incorrect because it does

not have the right middle sound. Option B is incorrect because it does not have the right beginning and middle sounds. In option D, the middle sound is correct, but the beginning and ending sounds are not.

9. B. picture of a clock
Option B is correct. The picture shows a clock. Option A is incorrect because the letters in *clock* do not stand for the sounds heard in the picture name *lamp*. Option C is incorrect because *lock* has the same middle and ending sounds as clock, but the beginning sound is different. Option D is incorrect because *bike* has different beginning and middle sounds than *clock*.

10. B. turtle
Option B is correct. The picture shows a turtle. Option A is incorrect. Snakes and turtles are different animals, and their names have different beginning, middle and ending sounds. Option C is incorrect because the beginning and middle sounds are different than the sounds in *turtle*. Option D is incorrect because *table* has different middle sounds than *turtle*.

Lesson 3 (pages 14–15)

1. B. 446 Sundown Pl.
Option B is correct. The street address is usually the second line of an address and contains the number of the building and the name of the street. Option A is incorrect because it is the name of the person to whom the address belongs. Option C is incorrect because it is the city. Option D is incorrect because it is the ZIP code.

2. A. Anna Rios
Option A is correct. The name of the person or company is usually the first line of an address. Option B is incorrect because it is the number of the building and the name of the street. Option C is incorrect because it is the name of the city. Option D is incorrect because it is the ZIP code.

3. C. St. Louis
Option C is correct. The name of the city is usually on the third line and is followed by the state and the ZIP code. Option A is incorrect because it is the name of the person. Option B is incorrect because it is the number of the building and the street name. Option D is incorrect because it is the ZIP code.

4. C. Miami
Option C is correct. The name of the city is usually on the third line and is followed by the state and the ZIP code. Option A is incorrect because it is the name of the person. Option B is incorrect because it is

the number of the building and the street name. Option D is incorrect because it is the ZIP code.

5. B. 1325 Penn Ct.
Option B is correct. The street address is usually the second line of an address and contains the number of the building and the name of the street. Option A is incorrect because it is the name of the person. Option C is incorrect because it is the city. Option D is incorrect because it is the ZIP code.

6. A. Tyrell Wilson
Option A is correct. The name of the person or company is usually the first line of an address. Option B is incorrect because it is the number of the building and the name of the street. Option C is incorrect because it is the city. Option D is incorrect because it is the ZIP code.

7. A. Elena Ochoa
Option A is correct. The name of the person or company is usually the first line of an address. Option B is incorrect because it is the number of the building and the name of the street. Option C is incorrect because it is the city. Option D is incorrect because it is the phone number.

8. C. Pittsburgh
Option C is correct. The name of the city is usually on the third line and is followed by the name of the state and the ZIP code. Option A is incorrect because it is the name of the person. Option B is incorrect because it is the number of the building and the street name. Option D is incorrect because it is the phone number.

9. D. (412) 555-1234
Option D is correct. The phone number contains three sets of numbers. The first set is the area code, the second is the specific area or city, and the third identifies the person who has that number. Option A is incorrect because it is the name of the person. Option B is incorrect because it is the number of the building and the street name. Option C is incorrect because it is the city.

10. C. Wilmington
Option C is correct. The name of the city is usually on the third line and is followed by the name of the state and the ZIP code. Option A is incorrect because it is the name of the person. Option B is incorrect because it is the number of the building and the street name. Option D is incorrect because it is the ZIP code.

11. A. Richard McCloud
Option A is correct. The name of the person or company is usually the first line of an address. Option B is incorrect because it is

the number of the building and the name of the street. Option C is incorrect because it is the city. Option D is incorrect because it is the ZIP code.

12. B. 10023 Maple St.
Option B is correct. The street address is usually the second line of an address and contains the number of the building and the name of the street. Option A is incorrect because it is the name of the person. Option C is incorrect because it is the city. Option D is incorrect because it is the ZIP code.

Lesson 4 (pages 18–19)

1. B. beautiful
Option B is correct because *beautiful* means "pretty"; it tells about the flowers. Options A, C, and D are incorrect because the words *shy, cold,* and *clean* do not tell what flowers are like.

2. A. narrow
Option A is correct because *narrow* means "not wide"; it tells about the path. Options B, C, and D are incorrect because the words *loud, tall,* and *eager* would not be used to tell what a path is like.

3. D. played
Option D is correct because *played* means "took part in"; it is an action word that tells what you do with a game. Options A, B, and C are incorrect because the words *smelled, walked,* and *turned* do not tell actions that are related to a game.

4. A. late
Option A is correct because *late* means "not on time"; it can tell about a bus. Options B, C, and D are incorrect because the words *proud, dim,* and *tired* do not tell what a bus is like.

5. C. name
Option C is correct because the word *name* is linked to *Kate*. It tells what the sentence is about. Options A, B, and D are incorrect because the words *neck, color,* and *candy* do not refer to *Kate*.

6. B. loud
Option B is correct because *loud* means "a great sound"; it tells about the noise. Options A, C, and D are incorrect because the words *pink, round,* and *hot* do not tell what a noise is like.

7. C. grass
Option C is correct because the word *grass* names a kind of plant that is green. Options A, B, and D are incorrect because the words *cloud, dirt,* and *squirrel* name things that are not usually green.

8. B. deep

Option B is correct because *deep* means "a long way down"; it tells about the pool, which is a body of water. Options A, C, and D are incorrect because the words *clever*, *easy*, and *slow* do not tell what a pool is like.

9. D. washed

Option D is correct because *washed* is an action word that means "cleaned"; it tells something you can do to windows. Options A, B, and C are incorrect because the words *folded*, *kissed*, and *parked* tell actions that you would not do to windows.

10. C. baked

Option C is correct because *baked* is an action word that means "cooked in an oven"; it tells something you do when you make a cake. Options A, B, and D are incorrect because the words *called*, *closed*, and *hugged* do not tell actions you would do to make a cake.

11. B. brother

Option B is correct because *brother* names a person who could be brave, or without fear. Options A, C, and D are incorrect because the words *pocket*, *bedroom*, and *hand* name things that would not be called brave.

12. D. filled

Option D is correct because *filled* is an action word that means "made full"; it tells something you can do to a pail, or bucket. Options A, B, and C are incorrect because the words *melted*, *smiled*, and *raked* do not tell actions that you would do with a pail.

Lesson 5 (pages 22–23)

1. A. Donna

Option A is correct because *Donna* names the person who dropped the bag. Option B is incorrect because *travel* tells about the bag. Option C is incorrect because *bag* is what she dropped. Option D is incorrect because the *scale* is where she dropped it.

2. A. Mrs. Kim

Option A is correct because *Mrs. Kim* names the person who took a paycheck to the bank. Option B is incorrect because *took* tells what Mrs. Kim did. Option C is incorrect because *paycheck* is what she took. Option D is incorrect because *bank* is where she took her paycheck.

3. B. bike

Option B is correct because *bike* names the thing Juan rides. Option A is incorrect because *Juan* tells who rides the bike. Option C is incorrect because *work* names the place he rides to. Option D is incorrect

because, as part of the phrase *every day*, it tells when Juan rides.

4. D. Taylor

Option D is correct because *Taylor* names the person who paid the taxes. Option A is incorrect because *income* tells about the taxes. Option B is incorrect because *taxes* names what she paid. Option C is incorrect because, as part of the phrase *before the deadline*, it tells when she paid the taxes.

5. C. peppers

Option C is correct because *peppers* names the things the cooks chopped. Option A is incorrect because *cooks* tells who chopped the peppers. Option B is incorrect because *green* tells about the peppers. Option D is incorrect because *salsa* tells what the cooks made.

6. B. friends

Option B is correct because *friends* name the ones who joined the army. Option A is incorrect because *three* tells how many friends there are. Option C is incorrect because *army* is what they joined. Option D is incorrect because *together* is how they joined it.

7. C. customer

Option C is correct because *customer* names the person who asked for water. Option A is incorrect because *more* tells about the water. Option B is incorrect because *water* is what the customer asked for. Option D is incorrect because *server* is the person whom the customer asked.

8. B. explorers

Option B is correct because *explorers* names the ones who found things. Option A is incorrect because *bold* describes the explorers. Option C is incorrect because *things* are what the explorers found. Option D is incorrect because *interesting* describes the things.

9. B. Kateri

Option B is correct because *Kateri* names the person who takes shopping bags to the store. Option A is incorrect because *bags* tells what she takes. Option C is incorrect because *store* names the place where she takes them. Option D is incorrect because *shopping* tells what kind of bags.

10. B. clock

Option B is correct because *clock* names the thing Tamika set. Option A is incorrect because *Tamika* names the person who set the clock. Options C and D are incorrect because together, the words *six o'clock* tell what time she set the clock for.

11. C. door

Option C is correct because *door* names the thing the dog scratched. Option A is incorrect because *dog* names the animal that scratched. Option B is incorrect because *to go* describes why the dog scratched. Option D is incorrect because *outside* names where the dog wanted to go.

12. D. Peter

Option D is correct because *Peter* names the person who keeps tools. Option A is incorrect because *garage* tells where Peter keeps the tools. Option B is incorrect because *tools* names what he keeps in the garage. Option C is incorrect because *power* tells what kind of tools.

Lesson 6 (pages 26–27)

1. D. (?)

Option D is correct. The sentence begins with *Where* and asks a question about the book. A reply or answer is expected. Option A is incorrect because this is not a sentence that tells a fact or gives a command. Option B is incorrect because a comma is not an end mark. Option C is incorrect because the sentence does not show strong feelings.

2. D. (?)

Option D is correct. This sentence begins with *What* and asks a question about someone's name. Option A is incorrect because this is not a sentence that tells a fact or gives a command. Option B is incorrect because a comma is not an end mark. Option C is incorrect because the sentence does not show strong feelings.

3. A. (.)

Option A is correct. This sentence tells the fact that Maddie was on time for work. Option B is incorrect because a comma is not an end mark. Option C is incorrect because this sentence does not show strong feelings. Option D is incorrect because this is not a question about Maddie, being on time, or work.

4. D. (?)

Option D is correct. This sentence begins with *Who* and asks a question. Option A is incorrect because this is not a sentence that tells a fact or gives a command. Option B is incorrect because a comma is not an end mark. Option C is incorrect because the sentence does not show strong feelings.

5. C. (!)

Option C is correct. This sentence shows surprise or excitement. The exclamation point shows the speaker's strong feeling or reaction. Option A is incorrect because, although this sentence gives a command, it is said or written to show strong feelings. Option B is incorrect because a comma is not an end mark. Option D is incorrect because this is not a question.

6. D. (?)
Option D is correct. This sentence begins with *When* and asks a question about putting gas in the car. Option A is incorrect because this is not a sentence that tells a fact or gives a command. Option B is incorrect because a comma is not an end mark. Option C is incorrect because the sentence does not show strong feelings.

7. A. (.)
Option A is correct. This sentence tells a fact: Jared shut his eyes. Option B is incorrect because a comma is not an end mark. Option C is incorrect because this sentence does not show strong feelings. Option D is incorrect because this is not a question.

8. C. (!)
Option C is correct. The exclamation point shows the importance of making the call right now. The sentence is said or written with strong feeling. Option A is incorrect because the sentence does not tell a fact. The sentence gives a command with strong feeling, so a period is not the best end mark. Option B is incorrect because a comma is not an end mark. Option D is incorrect because this is not a question.

9. D. (?)
Option D is correct. This sentence begins with *How* and asks a question about eggs. It can be answered. Option A is incorrect because this is not a sentence that tells a fact. Option B is incorrect because a comma is not an end mark. Option C is incorrect because the sentence does not show strong feelings.

10. A. (.)
Option A is correct. This sentence tells a fact: Carlos bought milk. Option B is incorrect because a comma is not an end mark. Option C is incorrect because this sentence does not show strong feelings. Option D is incorrect because this is not a question about Carlos or milk.

11. D. (?)
Option D is correct. This sentence begins with a form of the word *Do* and asks a question about the corn. A reply or answer to the question is expected. Option A is incorrect because this is not a sentence that tells a fact or gives a command. Option B is incorrect because a comma is not an

end mark. Option C is incorrect because the sentence does not show strong feelings.

12. D. (?)
Option D is correct. This sentence begins with the word *Who* and asks a question about which person or persons want to order lunch. Option A is incorrect because this is not a sentence that tells a fact or gives a command. Option B is incorrect because a comma is not an end mark. Option C is incorrect because the sentence does not show strong feelings.

13. A. (.)
Option A is correct. This sentence gives a command. It tells someone to do something. Option B is incorrect because a comma is not an end mark. Option C is incorrect because this sentence does not show strong feelings. Option D is incorrect because this sentence does not ask someone to get the mail, it tells them to do so.

14. D. (?)
Option D is correct. This sentence asks if we have arrived where we were going. It is a question. A reply or answer is expected. Option A is incorrect because this is not a sentence that tells a fact or gives a command. Option B is incorrect because a comma is not an end mark. Option C is incorrect because the sentence does not show strong feelings.

15. D. (?)
Option D is correct. This sentence begins with *Where* and asks a question about the location of the men's soccer game. Option A is incorrect because this is not a sentence that tells a fact or gives a command. Option B is incorrect because a comma is not an end mark. Option C is incorrect because the sentence does not show strong feelings.

16. A. (.)
Option A is correct. This sentence gives a command. It tells someone to do something. Option B is incorrect because a comma is not an end mark. Option C is incorrect because this sentence does not show strong feelings. Option D is incorrect because this is not a question about keys.

Check In 1 (pages 29–33)

1. C. E
Option C is correct. *E* is the letter that comes between *D* and *F*. Option A is incorrect because, in the alphabet, *B* comes before *C*, the first letter listed here. Options B and D are incorrect because *H* and *M* come after *G*, the last letter listed.

2. D. K
Option D is correct. *K* is the letter that comes between *J* and *L*. Options A and B are incorrect because *H* and *C* come before *J*. Option C is incorrect because *O* comes after *N*.

3. B. Y
Option B is correct. The letter that comes between *X* and *Z* is *Y*. Options A, C, and D are incorrect because *S*, *U*, and *Q* come before *V*.

4. A. T
Option A is correct. *T* is the letter that comes between *S* and *U*. Option B is incorrect because *P* comes before *Q*. Options C and D are incorrect because *X* and *V* come after *U*.

5. B. P
Option B is correct. The letter *P* comes between letters *O* and *Q*. Options A and D are incorrect because *M* and *L* come before *N*. Option C is incorrect because *S* comes after *R*.

6. B. J
Option B is correct. The letter that comes between *I* and *K* is *J*. Options A, C, and D are incorrect because *C*, *D*, and *G* all come before *H*.

7. B. lock
Option B is correct. The word *lock* names the picture. Options A, C, and D are incorrect because they do not name the picture.

8. A. hand
Option A is correct. The word *hand* names the picture. Options B, C, and D are incorrect because they do not name the picture.

9. A. ladder
Option A is correct. The word *ladder* names the picture. Options B, C, and D are incorrect because they do not name the picture.

10. C. bird
Option C is correct. *Bird* is the word that names the picture. Options A, B, and D are incorrect because they do not name the picture.

11. C. picture of a tiger
Option C is correct. It is the picture that goes with the word *tiger*. Option A is the picture of a car tire. Option B is the picture of a pepper. Option D is the picture of a dog.

12. C. teacher
Option C is correct. *Teacher* names the person who gave the book. Option A is incorrect because *student* names the person who received the book. Option B is incorrect because *book* is what was given. Option D is incorrect because *new* describes the book.

13. D. pie

Option D is correct. *Pie* names what was made. Option A is incorrect because *wife* names the person for whom the pie was made. Option B is incorrect because *Kent* names the person who made the pie. Option C is incorrect because *peach* describes the type of pie.

14. D. Brianna

Option D is correct. *Brianna* names the person who left the keys. Option A is incorrect because *keys* names what was left in the coat pocket. Option B is incorrect because *pocket* is where the keys were left. Option C is incorrect because *coat* describes the pocket where the keys were left.

15. A. towels

Option A is correct. *Towels* names what was stored. Option B is incorrect because *closet* names the place where the towels were stored. Option C is incorrect because *Alice* names the person who stored the towels. Option D is incorrect because *clean* describes the towels.

16. B. Manuel

Option B is correct. *Manuel* names the person who listened. Option A is incorrect because *radio* names what was listened to. Option C is incorrect because *earphones* names the things he listened with. Option D is incorrect because *his* tells who owned the earphones.

17. A. neighbors

Option A is correct. *Neighbors* names the people who worked. Option B is incorrect because *together* describes how the people worked. Option C is incorrect because *to clean* tells why they worked. Option D is incorrect because *park* names what was cleaned.

18. B. dog

Option B is correct. The sentence is missing a word that names something that can be fed. Options A, C, and D are incorrect because the words name things are not fed.

19. A. car

Option A is correct. The sentence is missing a word that names something that can go fast. Options B, C, and D are incorrect because they are not things that can go fast.

20. C. cold

Option C is correct. The sentence is missing a word that describes snow, and snow is cold. Options A, B, and D are incorrect because the words cannot be used to describe snow.

21. D. song

Option D is correct. The sentence is missing a word that names a thing that can be sung.

Options A, B, and C are incorrect because they do not name things that can be sung.

22. B. toolbox

Option B is correct. The sentence needs a word that names something that can be locked. Toolboxes can be locked to protect tools that are kept inside. Options A, C, and D are incorrect because they name things that cannot be locked.

23. C. glass

Option C is correct. The sentence is missing a word that names something that can be broken. Glass can be broken. Options A, B, and D are incorrect because they name things that cannot be broken.

24. B. 5685 Pearl St.

Option B is correct. The house or building number and street name are located on the second line of an address. Option A is incorrect because it is the name of the person. Option C is incorrect because it is the name of the city. Option D is incorrect because it is the ZIP code.

25. A. Anthony Hernandez

Option A is correct. Anthony Hernandez is the name of the person who is at the address. The name is the first line of an address. Option B is incorrect because it is the street address. Option C is incorrect because it is the city. Option D is incorrect because it is the ZIP code.

26. C. Nashville

Option C is correct. Nashville is the name of the city. It is the first part of the third line of an address, which contains the city, state, and ZIP code. Option A is incorrect because it is the name of the person. Option B is incorrect because it is the street address. Option D is incorrect because it is the ZIP code.

27. D. (?)

Option D is correct. This sentence asks what Rosa had for lunch. It is a question that can be answered. Option A is incorrect because this is not a sentence that states a fact or is a command. Option B is incorrect because a comma is not an end mark. Option C is incorrect because this sentence is not an exclamation.

28. A. (.)

Option A is correct. This sentence states a fact: the truck is in the garage. Option B is incorrect because a comma is not an end mark. Option C is incorrect because this sentence is not an exclamation. Option D is incorrect because this sentence is not a question that can be answered.

29. D. (?)

Option D is correct. The sentence begins

with *Where* and is a question. Option A is incorrect because the sentence does not state a fact or give a command. Option B is incorrect because a comma is not an end mark. Option C is incorrect because the sentence is not an exclamation.

Lesson 7 (pages 38–39)

1. A. Tess

Option A is correct. *Tess* names the person who left her sweater on the bus. Option B is incorrect because *blue* describes the sweater. Option C is incorrect because *sweater* is what she left. Option D is incorrect because it names a thing and, as part of the phrase *on the bus*, it tells where she left it.

2. D. Jesse

Option D is correct. *Jesse* names the person who wrote the check. Option A is incorrect because the word *repairs* names the things for which Jesse wrote the check. Option B is incorrect because *auto* tells what kind of repairs. Option C is incorrect because *check* is what Jesse wrote.

3. B. pitcher

Option B is correct. The word *pitcher* names the thing that slipped. Option A is incorrect because *water* tells what kind of pitcher. Option C is incorrect because the word *hands* names the things that are holding the pitcher. Option D is incorrect because *Amanda's* tells whose hands they are.

4. C. tickets

Option C is correct. The word *tickets* names the things my brother bought. Option A is incorrect because *brother* names the person who bought the tickets. Option B is incorrect because *two* tells how many tickets. Option D is incorrect because *concert* names a thing and, as part of the phrase *for the concert*, it tells why he bought the tickets.

5. A. George

Option A is correct. *George* names the person who took a walk. Option B is incorrect because *brisk* tells what kind of walk. Option C is incorrect because *walk* tells what George took. Option D is incorrect because *block* names a thing and, as part of the phrase *around the block*, it tells where he walked.

6. C. leak

Option C is correct. The word *leak* names the thing Keisha discovered. Option A is incorrect because *Keisha* names the person who discovered the leak. Option B is incorrect because *slow* describes the leak. Option D is incorrect because *tire* names a thing and, as part of the phrase *in her tire*, it tells where the leak was found.

7. A. Dr. Abrams

Option A is correct. *Dr. Abrams* names the person who reviewed the x-rays. Option B is incorrect because the word *x-rays* names the things that Dr. Abrams reviewed. Option C is incorrect because *injured* describes the ankle. Option D is incorrect because *ankle* names the thing shown in the x-rays.

8. B. mixed

Option B is correct. The word *mixed* is an action word that tells what Sylvie did. Option A is incorrect because *Sylvie* names the person who mixed the walnuts into the dough. Option C is incorrect because *walnuts* names what was mixed into the dough. Option D is incorrect because *cookie* tells what kind of dough Sylvie mixed.

9. C. museum

Option C is correct. The word *museum* names what Jared explored. Option A is incorrect because *Jared* names the person who explored the museum. Option B is incorrect because *history* tells what kind of museum. Option D is incorrect because the word *sons* names the persons Jared was with.

10. A. workers

Option A is correct. The word *workers* names the people who fixed the sidewalk. Option B is incorrect because *broken* describes the sidewalk. Option C is incorrect because *sidewalk* names the thing the workers fixed. Option D is incorrect because *cement* is the material they used to fix the sidewalk.

11. C. tree

Option C is correct. The word *tree* names the thing the squirrels climb. Option A is incorrect because the word *squirrels* names the animals that do the climbing. Option B is incorrect because *tall* tells what kind of tree they climb. Option D is incorrect because *yard* names the place where the tree is.

12. B. tomatoes

Option B is correct. The word *tomatoes* names what Emil added to the stew. Option A is incorrect because *Emil* names the person who added something to the stew. Option C is incorrect because *beef* tells what kind of stew. Option D is incorrect because *stew* names the thing to which Emil added the tomatoes.

Lesson 8 (pages 42–43)

1. B. scent

Option B is correct. A candle that smells nice has a lovely scent. Options A and C are incorrect because *glow* and *shade* are related to the sight of the candle, not to its smell. Option D is incorrect because a *stink* is a bad smell, not a lovely smell.

2. C. panic

Option C is correct. If a bike is missing, the owner might feel fear and alarm, or panic. Option A is incorrect because a clash is a loud noise or a disagreement. Options B and D are incorrect because neither *struggle* nor *relax* name an action that is a logical response to a missing bike.

3. C. swell

Option C is correct. The word *if* shows a cause-and-effect relationship. If Ed does not ice his ankle, it will swell. Options A and B are incorrect because forgetting to ice an ankle would not cause Ed's ankle to shrink or become scratched. Option D is incorrect because forgetting to ice an injury would likely be harmful; it would not cause the condition to improve.

4. D. uneasy

Option D is correct. A person who is afraid of water would probably feel uncomfortable, or uneasy, driving over water on a bridge. Options A and B are incorrect because a person who is afraid does not necessarily feel angry or confused. Option C is incorrect because a person who is afraid of water is not likely to feel comfortable driving over it.

5. B. prepare

Option B is correct. The phrase *study hard* explains what someone should do to prepare for a test. Option A is incorrect because forgetting would make someone do poorly on a test. Option C is incorrect because swallowing would not affect how you perform on a test. Option D is incorrect because *revolt* means "to rebel against authority"; it doesn't make sense in the sentence.

6. A. experience

Option A is correct. Seeing the Grand Canyon in person is one way to experience it. Options B, C, and D are incorrect because they do not have to do with enjoying the Grand Canyon: *exchange* means "to trade"; *imitate* means "to try to be like"; *spoil* means "to destroy the value of a thing."

7. B. fussy

Option B is correct. The sentence compares the fussy, or hard-to-please, son to the easy-to-please daughter. The word *but* is a clue to the contrast in the sentence. Options A, C, and D are incorrect because *friendly, clumsy,* and *eager* do not have meanings opposite to the phrase *easy to please.*

8. C. include

Option C is correct. The word *include* means "to make someone part of a group." If Ralph is invited to play in the game, he can play first base. Options A, B, and D are incorrect because they do not make sense in the sentence: *capture* means "to take as a prisoner"; *upset* means "to disturb"; *believe* means "to trust."

9. D. debate

Option D is correct. When people *debate* an issue, they discuss reasons for and against their opinions. Options A, B, and C are incorrect because they do not fit the meaning of the sentence: *check* means "to examine something"; *practice* means "to train"; *score* means "to make points in a game."

10. B. gasp

Option B is correct. When people are surprised by something, they sometimes gasp, or take a gulp of air. Everyone in the crowd is astonished, or surprised, by the news; it makes sense that they might gasp. Options A and C are incorrect because, while people might whisper to each other at bad news or squawk in anger, neither word expresses surprise as well as the word *gasp.* Option D is incorrect because a *signal* is a warning. It is not a likely response to an announcement.

11. C. icy

Option C is correct because the snowstorm would cause the road to be icy, causing the truck to slide. Options A, B, and D are incorrect because these words could be used to describe a road, but they do not describe conditions caused by a snowstorm.

12. A. improve

Option A is correct. A company generally tries to improve, or better, its products and services so that they can attract more customers. Option B, C, and D are incorrect because they do not make sense in this sentence: *collect* means "to gather together"; *interrupt* means "stop from time to time"; *require* means "need."

Lesson 9 (pages 46–47)

1. B. *Act* surprised even though you know about the party.

Option B is correct. As in the bracketed sentence, option B uses *act* as an action word meaning "to behave." Option A is incorrect because it uses *act* as an action word meaning "to do something." Option C is incorrect because it uses *act* to name one of the main parts of a play. Option D is incorrect because it uses *act* to name behavior that is insincere.

2. D. Will you *repeat* what you said a little louder?

Option D is correct. As in the bracketed sentence, option D uses *repeat* as an action word meaning "to say the same thing again." Option A is incorrect because it uses *repeat* to mean "a rerun." Option B is incorrect because it uses *repeat* to describe customers who come back to the same place. Option C is incorrect because it uses *repeat* as an action word meaning "to appear or occur again."

3. A. Sam hung a chin-up *bar* in the basement.

Option A is correct. As in the bracketed sentence, option A uses *bar* to name a straight, long piece of wood or metal. Option B is incorrect because it uses *bar* to name a counter at which food or drinks are served. Option C is incorrect because it uses *bar* to name a standard. Option D is incorrect because it uses *bar* as an action word meaning "to shut out."

4. A. Rico used a *plate* of glass to make a tabletop.

Option A is correct. As in the bracketed sentence, option A uses *plate* as a word meaning "a sheet of material." Option B is incorrect because *plate* names a dish. Option C is incorrect because *plate* names a schedule of things to deal with. Option D is incorrect because it uses *plate* as an action word meaning "to cover with a layer of metal."

5. B. Arthur is worried about the *shape* of his finances.

Option B is correct. As in the bracketed sentence, option B uses *shape* as a word meaning "state, or condition." Option A is incorrect because it uses *shape* as a word meaning "form." Option C is incorrect because it uses *shape* as an action word meaning "to mold." Option D is incorrect because it uses *shape* as an action word meaning "to direct."

6. D. The park rules were printed on a *sign* near the entrance.

Option D is correct. As in the bracketed sentence, option D uses *sign* to name a board showing written information. Option A is incorrect because it uses *sign* as an action word meaning "to write." Option B is incorrect because it uses *sign* to name a motion that stands for something. Option C is incorrect because it uses *sign* to name something that shows something else.

7. D. Sergio left a *note* saying he would be home soon.

Option D is correct. As in the bracketed sentence, option D uses *note* as a word meaning "a memo." Option A is incorrect because it uses *note* as an action word meaning "to notice." Option B is incorrect because it uses *note* to name a musical tone. Option C is incorrect because it uses *note* as an action word meaning "to record in writing."

8. B. Jamie's *net* pay was just enough to cover food and rent.

Option B is correct. As in the bracketed sentence, option B uses *net* to describe the amount of pay that is left after taxes and other deductions. Option A is incorrect because it uses *net* to name a device for catching fish. Option C is incorrect because it uses *net* as an action word meaning "to score." Option D is incorrect because it uses *net* to name a thing that divides a volleyball court in half.

9. A. I lost one *pound* after running for a few days.

Option A is correct. As in the bracketed sentence, option A uses *pound* to name a unit of weight. Option B is incorrect because it uses *pound* as an action word meaning "to hit hard with your fists." Option C is incorrect because it uses *pound* to name an enclosure for animals. Option D is incorrect because it uses *pound* as an action word meaning "to beat, or throb."

10. C. Daria wants to *frame* the photo and display it.

Option C is correct. As in the bracketed sentence, option C uses *frame* as an action word meaning "to put a border around." Option A is incorrect because it uses *frame* as an action word meaning "to plan and organize." Option B is incorrect because it uses *frame* to name the basic structure of a house. Option D is incorrect because it uses *frame* to name the physical makeup of a body.

11. D. Be careful not to *slip* on the wet floor.

Option D is correct. As in the bracketed sentence, option D uses *slip* as an action word meaning "skid, or slide." Option A is incorrect because it uses *slip* as an action word meaning "to go quietly." Option B is incorrect because it uses *slip* to name a cover. Option C is incorrect because it uses *slip* as an action word meaning "to pass out of a person's memory."

12. C. You may have a long *wait* to see the doctor.

Option C is correct. As in the bracketed sentence, option C is correct because the sentence uses *wait* to name a period of time in which activity is stopped until something happens. Option A is incorrect because it uses *wait* as an action word meaning "to stay undone, or to be put off." Option B is incorrect because it uses *wait* as an action word meaning "to serve a customer." Option D is incorrect because it uses *wait* as an action word meaning "to stay in place until something happens."

Lesson 10 (pages 50–51)

1. A. 1:03 P.M.

Option A is correct. The low tide in the afternoon is at 1:03 P.M. Option B is incorrect because it is the time for low tide in the morning. Option C is incorrect because it is the time for high tide on June 4. Option D is incorrect because it is the time for low tide on the afternoon of July 4.

2. C. June 4.

Option C is correct. In the *Sunrise* column, the earliest time listed is 6:23 A.M. If you follow the row to the left of the schedule, you'll find the date *June 4.* Option A is incorrect because the time of 7:09 A.M. is later than 6:23 A.M. Options B and C are incorrect because the sun also rose later on those dates than it did on June 4.

3. D. July 4.

Option D is correct. In the *Sunset* column, the latest time listed is 8:28 P.M. If you follow the row to the left of the schedule, you'll find the date *July 4.* Option A is incorrect because the April 4 sunset is at 7:44 P.M., which is earlier than 8:28 P.M. Options B and C are incorrect because the sun also set earlier on those dates than it did on July 4.

4. C. 7:10 P.M.

Option C is correct. The first *High Tide* column lists times in the morning. The second *High Tide* column lists times in the evening. 7:10 P.M. is in the row for May 4. Option A is incorrect because it shows the time of the high tide in the morning. Option B is incorrect because is shows the time of the sunset on May 4. Option D is incorrect because it is the time of the afternoon low tide on May 4.

5. A. April 4.

Option A is correct. The sun sets at 7:44 P.M. on April 4. This is before 8:00 P.M. Options B, C, and D are incorrect because the sun sets after 8:00 P.M. on those days.

6. D. 2:13 P.M.

Option D is correct. The afternoon low tide on July 4 is at 2:13. Option A is incorrect because it is the time of the morning low tide on July 4. Option B is incorrect because it is the time of the afternoon low tide on April 4. Option C is incorrect because it is the time of the evening high tide on July 4.

7. A. Mystery Book Club.

Option A is correct. It is the only option that mentions books. Options B, C, and D are incorrect because the activities do not include reading for enjoyment. The key to the answer is in the words *like to read* and *most likely*. People who like to read would *most likely* pick the book club.

8. D. Your Home Workshop
Option D is correct. There is a fee of $5 for organizers. Options A, B, and C are incorrect. There are no fees listed in the schedule for these activities.

9. A. Tuesday at 7:00 P.M.
Option A is correct. The Job and Career Counseling begins at 7:00 P.M. Option B is when the Your Home Workshop begins. Option C is when the Mystery Book Club begins. Option D is when Family Movie Night begins.

10. C. Your Home Workshop
Option C is correct. The schedule information on Your Home Workshop tells about getting organized and getting rid of clutter, which is information that can help you to organize a closet. Options A, B, and D are incorrect. None of them is about getting organized.

11. A. once in the month.
Option A is correct. The information in the right-hand column tells that the Bloodmobile is at the library on the first Thursday of each month. That is one day per month. Options B, C, and D are incorrect because the Bloodmobile does not come to the library every week or on weekends.

12. A. one
Option A is correct. Your Home Workshop is on Saturday. The weekend includes Saturday and Sunday. Options B, C, and D are incorrect because there is one activity on the weekend.

Lesson 11 (pages 54–55)

1. A. august
Option A is correct. *August* is the name of the eighth month of the year. Begin the names of months with capital letters. Options B, C, and D are incorrect because they are common nouns.

2. A. mrs.
Option A is correct. *Mrs.* is a title that comes before a name. Titles such as these should be capitalized. Options B, C, and D are incorrect because they are common nouns.

3. B. april
Option B is correct. *April* is the name of the fourth month of the year. Begin the names of months with capital letters. Options A and D are incorrect because *rain* and *business* are common nouns. Option C is incorrect because *hurt* names an action.

4. B. senator
Option B is correct. *Senator* is a title that comes before the personal last name *Sage*. Titles that come before names are capitalized. Options A, C, and D are incorrect because they are common nouns.

5. D. professor
Option D is correct. *Professor* is a title that comes before the personal name *Julie Chang*. Titles that come before names are capitalized. Options A and B are incorrect because they are common nouns. Option C is incorrect because it is an action word, not a proper noun.

6. D. rugby
Option D is correct. *Rugby* is the name of a town, so it begins with a capital letter. Options A and C are incorrect because they are common nouns. Option B is incorrect because the word *doctor's* is used to describe the office where Manny's job is. In this case, the word *doctor's* is not part of a title and is not part of a proper noun.

7. A. pattis
Option A is correct. The last name *Pattis* refers to a specific family, so it is a proper noun. Options B and C are common nouns. Option D is incorrect because *officer* is used as a common noun in the sentence, not as a title.

8. D. july
Option D is correct. *July* is the name of the seventh month of the year. The names of the months are capitalized. Option A is incorrect because it is not a noun. Options B and C are incorrect because they are common nouns.

9. D. lieutenant
Option D is correct. A military title, such as *lieutenant*, is capitalized when it comes before a name. Options A and B are incorrect because they are common nouns. Option C is incorrect because it used as a common noun in the sentence, not as a title.

10. C. governor
Option C is correct. The name *J. K. Regis* has the title *governor* before it. A title that comes before a name begins with a capital letter. Options A, B and D are incorrect because they are common nouns.

11. A. january
Option A is correct. *January* is the name of the first month of the year. Begin the names of months with capital letters. Options B and D are incorrect because they are common nouns. Option C is incorrect because the word *shoveling* describes an action.

12. D. cleveland
Option D is correct. *Cleveland* is the name of a city. The names of cities begin with capital letters. Options A and C are incorrect because they are common nouns. Option B is incorrect because it is an action word, not a proper noun.

13. B. nurse
Option B is correct. In this sentence, *nurse* is a title that comes before the name *Keller*. A title that comes before a person's name begins with a capital letter. Options A, C, and D are incorrect because they are common nouns.

14. C. naples
Option C is correct. The names of cities begin with capital letters. Naples is a city in Italy. Options A and D are incorrect because they are common nouns. Option B is incorrect because *born* is an action word, not a proper noun.

15. B. florida
Option B is correct. The names of states begin with capital letters. Florida is a state. Options A and C are incorrect because they are action words. Option D is incorrect because it is a common noun.

16. C. march
Option C is correct. *March* is the name of the third month of the year. The months of the year always begin with capital letters. Options A, B, and D are incorrect because they are common nouns.

Lesson 12 (pages 58–59)

1. B. (,)
Option B is correct. The boots are described by three words in a list. Commas are used to separate the words in a list of three or more things. The first comma goes between the words *heavy* and *wet,* and the last comma goes before the word *and*. Options A, C, and D are end marks. End marks do not punctuate the middle of a list.

2. D. (?)
Option D is correct. The sentence asks a question. The word *Where* is a clue that the sentence is a question. A question ends with a question mark. Option A is a period (.). It ends a statement or command. Option B is a comma (,). Commas are used inside a sentence to separate words. Option C is an exclamation point (!). It ends a sentence that shows strong feelings.

3. B. (,)

Option B is correct. The sentence is a list of three actions. Each action is a group of words. The comma separates groups of words: *pay bills, walk the dog,* and *bake a cake.* Options A, C, and D are end marks. End marks do not punctuate the middle of a list.

4. D. (?)

Option D is correct. The sentence asks a question. A question ends with a question mark. Option A is a period (.). It ends a statement or command. Option B is a comma (,). Commas are used inside a sentence to separate words. Option C is an exclamation point (!). It ends a sentence that shows strong feelings.

5. B. (,)

Option B is correct. The sentence is a list of three actions. Each action is one word. The comma separates each action: *reads, bikes, and sews.* Options A, C, and D are incorrect because they are end marks.

6. B. (,)

Option B is correct. The sentence tells about three things that an apartment needs. A comma needs to separate *a lamp* from *a stool.* Options A, C, and D are incorrect because they are end marks. End marks are not used in the middle of a list.

7. B. (,)

Option B is correct. The comma before the word *and* shows that all three words describe the weather. Options A, C, and D are end marks. End marks do not punctuate the middle of a list.

8. D. (?)

Option D is correct. The sentence asks a question. The word *Who* is a clue that the sentence is a question. A question ends with a question mark. Option A is a period (.). It ends a sentence or command. Option B is a comma (,). Commas are used inside a sentence to separate words. Option C is an exclamation point (!). It ends a sentence that shows strong feelings.

9. B. (,)

Option B is correct. The sentence begins with a list of four names. A comma separates each name. The sentence names the four people who hiked along the lake. Options A, C, and D are end marks. End marks do not punctuate the middle of a list.

10. B. (,)

Option B is correct. The sentence describes the actions of three people on a Sunday. A comma is used to separate each person's action. A comma separates Magda's action from Ben's. Another comma is needed to separate the action of the speaker from

that of *Magda.* Options A, C, and D are end marks. End marks do not punctuate the middle of a list.

11. C. (!)

Option C is correct. The sentence is an exclamation. It shows strong feeling. Option A is incorrect because a period at the end of a sentence does not show strong feeling. Option B is a comma. A comma cannot end a sentence. Option D is incorrect because the sentence does not ask a question.

12. A. (.)

Option A is correct. The sentence is a command. A command ends with a period (.) Option B is incorrect because a comma is not used at the end of a sentence. Option C is incorrect because the sentence is not an exclamation. Option D is incorrect because the sentence is not a question.

13. B. (,)

Option B is correct. The sentence lists three things that the person drinks. A comma belongs after *water* and before the word *and.* Options A, C, and D are end marks. End marks do not punctuate the middle of a list.

14. B. (,)

Option B is correct. The sentence lists four things in the stew. A comma separates three or more items in a list. Options A, C, and D are end marks. End marks do not punctuate the middle of a list.

15. A. (.)

Option A is correct. The sentence is a command. A command ends with a period (.) Option B is incorrect because a comma is not used at the end of a sentence. Option C is incorrect because the sentence is not an exclamation. Option D is incorrect because the sentence is not a question.

16. B. (,)

Option B is correct. The sentence lists three colors. A comma separates the three things in a list. Options A, C, and D are end marks. End marks do not punctuate the middle of a list.

Lesson 13 (pages 63–65)

1. C. cook

This sentence uses the present tense form of the verb to show repeating action. Option C is correct because *cook* is a present tense verb form that agrees with the plural subject *we.* Option A does not agree with the subject *we.* Option B is incorrect because it is an incomplete verb form. Option D is incorrect because it does not make sense in the sentence.

2. A. wants

Option A is correct because *wants* is a present tense verb form that fits an action that happens today and agrees with the subject *Rafael.* The subject is third-person singular *(he, she,* or *it). Want* is a regular verb. So the correct form of the present tense is *want + -s.* Options B and D are not present tense verb forms. Option C is the form of the present tense that is used with plural subjects or with the subjects *I* and *you.*

3. C. listen

Option C is correct because *listen* is the only verb form that agrees with the third-person plural subject *Bob and Terry. Listen* is the correct form of the present tense. Option A is the present tense verb form for a third-person singular subject. Options B and D are incorrect because they do not agree with the plural subject.

4. D. is

Option D is correct because it is the only verb form that agrees with the third-person singular subject *Lois.* The verb *be* is irregular; the correct present tense verb form is *is.* Option A is incorrect because *are* is the present tense form used with a plural subject, such as *you, we,* or *they.* Option B is incorrect because it is the base form of the verb *to be.* It is not used to express the present tense. Option C is incorrect because *am* is the present tense form used with the subject *I.*

5. C. am

Option C is correct because *am* is the only verb form that agrees with the subject *I.* The subject is first-person singular. *Am* is the correct verb form in the present tense. Option A is incorrect because *are* is the present tense plural, but the subject is singular. Option B is incorrect because it is the base form of the verb *to be.* It is not used to express the present tense. Option D is incorrect because *is* is the present tense form for a third-person singular subject *(he, she,* or *it).*

6. B. like

Option B is correct because *like* is the only verb form that agrees with the subject. The present tense is often used to show action that repeats over time. The subject *we* is first-person plural. *Like* is the present tense verb that agrees with the plural subject *we.* Option A is incorrect because *likes* is the present tense form that is used with the singular subjects *he, she,* and *it.* Options C and D are incorrect because they are not verbs in the present tense, and they do not agree with the plural subject *we.*

7. B. have
Option B is correct because it is the present tense verb that agrees with the subject *you*. The word *today* shows present tense. *Have* is an irregular verb with two forms in the present tense, *have* and *has*. *You* is a second-person subject. *Have* is used with the subject *you*. Option A is incorrect because *has* is the incorrect present tense form for the subject *you*. It is used with the singular subjects *he, she,* and *it*. Option C is not a present tense form of the verb *have*. Option D is an incomplete verb form.

8. D. plays
Option D is correct because *plays* is the only verb form that agrees with the subject *Aska*. The subject is third-person singular. The correct verb form of the simple present tense is *play + -s*. Option A is incorrect because it is an incomplete verb form. Option B is incorrect because it is not a verb form of *play*. Option C is incorrect because *play* does not agree with the subject.

9. A. deliver
Option A is correct because *deliver* is the only verb form that agrees with the subject *I*. The subject is first-person singular. *Deliver* is the correct form of the present tense. Option B is incorrect because it is the present tense form that goes with the single subject *he, she,* or *it*. Options C and D are incorrect because they are not present tense verb forms, and they do not agree with the subject *I*.

10. A. are
Option A is correct because *are* is the only verb form that agrees with the second-person subject *you*. *Are* is the correct verb form of the present tense. Option B is incorrect because it is the base form of the verb *be*. Option C is incorrect because *am* is the present tense form that is used with the subject *I*. Option D is incorrect because *is* is the verb form used with the subjects *he, she,* and *it*.

11. C. eats
Option C is correct because *eats* is the only verb form that agrees with the subject *who*. In questions, the word *who* acts like *he, she,* or *it*. So the subject *who* is third-person singular. The correct verb form of the present tense is *eat + -s*. Options A and D are incorrect because they are incomplete verb forms. Options B is incorrect because it doesn't agree with the subject.

12. B. have
Option B is correct because it is the only form of *have* that agrees with the subject. *Kids* is a third-person plural subject. Because the subject is plural, the correct present tense verb form is *have*. Option A is incorrect because *has* does not agree with the plural subject. Option C is incorrect because it is not a present tense form of the verb. Option D is incorrect because it is an incomplete verb form.

13. D. helps
Option D is correct because *helps* is the only verb form that agrees with the subject *librarian*. The subject is third-person singular. The correct present tense form of the verb is *help + -s*. Option A is incorrect because it is the present tense form of the verb that is used with the subjects *I, you, we,* and *they*. Option B is incorrect because it is an incomplete verb form. Option C is incorrect because it is not a present tense verb form.

14. A. want
Option A is correct because *want* is the only verb form that agrees with the subject *they*. *Want* is the present tense verb form used with a third-person plural subject. Option B is incorrect because is not a present tense verb form. Option C is incorrect because it is not a verb form of *want*. Option D is incorrect because it does not agree with the subject.

15. C. is
Option C is correct because *is* is the only verb form that agrees with *home*. The subject *home* is third-person singular. The correct present tense verb form is *is*. Option A is incorrect because *be* is the base form of the verb *be*. Option B is incorrect because it is the plural form of the present tense verb. Option D is incorrect because *am* is the first person form of the verb. It does not agree with the third-person singular subject.

16. B. move
Option B is correct because *move* is the only verb form that agrees with the plural subject *neighbors*. The sentence uses present tense to show repeated action. *Move* is the correct verb form of the present tense. Option A is incorrect because it does not agree with a plural subject. Option C is incorrect because it is not a present tense verb form. Option D is incorrect because it is an incomplete verb form.

17. A. want
Option A is correct because *want* is the only verb form that agrees with *I*. The subject *I* is first-person singular. *Want* is the correct present tense verb form. Option B is incorrect because it is a third-person verb form that does not agree with the subject. Option C is incorrect because it is an incomplete verb form. Option D is incorrect because is not a present tense verb form and it does not agree with the first-person singular subject.

18. C. are
Option C is correct because *are* is the only verb form that agrees with *we*. The subject *we* is first-person plural. *Are* is the correct present tense form of the verb *be*. Option A is incorrect because the present tense verb *is* is used with the singular subjects *he, she,* and *it*. Option B is incorrect because *am* is the present tense verb form used with the subject *I*. Option D is incorrect because it is the base form of the verb *be*.

19. D. has
Option D is correct because it is the only form of *have* that agrees with the singular subject *car*. In this sentence, present tense is used to tell a fact. *Has* is the present tense form of *have* that agrees with the subject. Option A is incorrect because *having* is an incomplete verb form. Option B is incorrect because it does not agree with the singular subject *car*. Option C is incorrect because it is not a present tense verb form.

20. B. finds
Option B is correct because *finds* is the only verb form that agrees with the singular subject *Chi*. The correct present tense verb form is *find + -s*. Option A is incorrect because it is an incomplete verb form. Option C is incorrect because it is not a present tense verb form and does not agree with the subject. Option D is incorrect because it does not agree with the third-person singular subject.

21. D. ends
Option D is correct because *ends* is the only verb form that agrees with the third-person singular subject *film*. The correct verb form of the simple present tense is *end + -s*. Option A is incorrect because it is the present tense form that goes with *I, you, we,* and *they*. Option B is incorrect because it is an incomplete verb form. Option C is incorrect because it is not a present tense verb form, and it does not agree with the singular subject *film*.

22. B. knows
Option B is correct because *knows* is the only verb form that agrees with *Hakan*. The subject *Hakan* is one person, so *Hakan* is third-person singular. *Knows* is the present tense verb form that agrees with a third-person singular subject. Option A is incorrect because it is not a present tense verb form and does not agree with the singular subject. Option C is incorrect because it is an incomplete verb form. Option D is the present tense verb form used with the subjects *I, you, we,* and *they*.

Lesson 14 (pages 69–71)

1. A. grew

Option A is correct. *Grew* is the past tense form of the irregular verb *grow*. Options B and D are incorrect because the verb forms do not agree with the subject *They*. Option C is incorrect because it is an incomplete verb form.

2. B. will see

Option B is correct. *Will see* is the future tense form of the verb *see*. Option A is incorrect because it is an incomplete verb form. Options C and D use the wrong verb form for the subject *I*.

3. C. drove

Option C is correct. *Drove* is the past tense form of the irregular verb *drive*. Options A and D are incorrect because they use the wrong verb form for the subject *Andrei*. Option B is not a verb form of *drive*.

4. B. chose

Option B is correct. *Chose* is the past tense form of the irregular verb *choose*. Options A and C are incorrect because they are incomplete verb forms. Option D is incorrect because it uses the wrong verb form for the subject *We*.

5. C. took

Option C is correct. *Took* is the past tense of the irregular verb *take*. Option A is incorrect because it is not a form of *take*. Option B is incorrect because it is an incomplete verb form. Option D is incorrect because it uses the wrong verb form for the subject *We*.

6. D. sat

Option D is correct. *Sat* is the past tense of the irregular verb *sit*. Option A is incorrect because it does not agree with the subject *Rebecca*. Options B and C are incorrect because they are not verb forms of *sit*.

7. B. caught

Option B is correct. *Caught* is the past tense of the irregular verb *catch*. Options A and C are incorrect because they are not verb forms of *catch*. Option D is incorrect because it is an incomplete verb form.

8. C. will swim

Option C is correct. *Will swim* is the future tense of *swim*. Options A and B are incorrect because they do not agree with the subject *Samuel*. Option D is incorrect because it is not a verb form of *swim*.

9. C. rose

Option C is correct. *Rose* is the past tense of the irregular verb *rise*. Options A and D are incorrect because they do not agree with the subject *sun*. Option B is incorrect because it is not a verb form of *rise*.

10. D. lost

Option D is correct. *Lost* is the past tense of the irregular verb *lose*. Options A and B are incorrect because they are not verb forms of *lose*. Option C is incorrect because it is an incomplete verb form.

11. A. thought

Option A is correct. *Thought* is the past tense of the irregular verb *think*. Option B is incorrect because it is not a verb form of *think*. Options C and D are incorrect because they do not agree with the subject *I*.

12. D. told

Option D is correct. *Told* is the past tense of the irregular verb *tell*. Option A is incorrect because it does not agree with the subject *Chet*. Options B and C are incorrect because they are not verb forms of *tell*.

13. A. heard

Option A is correct. *Heard* is the past tense of the irregular verb *hear*. Option B is incorrect because it is not a form of *hear*. Option C is incorrect because it does not agree with the subject *Jim*. Option D is incorrect because it is an incomplete verb form.

14. B. will wash

Option B is correct. *Will wash* is the future tense of *wash*. Options A and C are incorrect because they do not agree with the subject *Miguel*. Option D is incorrect because it is an incomplete verb form.

15. C. spoke

Option C is correct. *Spoke* is the past tense of the irregular verb *speak*. Options A and D are incorrect because they are incomplete verb forms. Option B is incorrect because it does not agree with the subject *I*.

16. A. ate

Option A is correct. *Ate* is the past tense of the irregular verb *eat*. Options B and D are incorrect because they are incomplete verb forms. Option C is incorrect because it does not agree with the subject *rabbit*.

17. C. saw

Option C is correct. *Saw* is the past tense of *see*. Options A and B are incorrect because they are incomplete verb forms. Option D is incorrect because it is not a verb form of *see*.

18. A. rang

Option A is correct. *Rang* is the past tense of the irregular verb *ring*. Option B is incorrect because it is an incomplete verb form. Option C is incorrect because it does not agree with the subject *Sherise*. Option D is incorrect because it is not a verb form of *ring*.

19. C. will ring

Option C is correct. *Will ring* is the future tense of *ring*. Option A is incorrect because it is an incomplete verb form. Option B is incorrect because it is not a verb form of *ring*. Option D is incorrect because it does not agree with the subject *I*.

20. B. swung

Option B is correct. *Swung* is the past tense of the irregular verb *swing*. Options A and D are incorrect because they do not agree with the subject *Ruben*. Option C is incorrect because it is an incomplete verb form.

21. C. wrote

Option C is correct. *Wrote* is the past tense of the irregular verb *write*. Option A is incorrect because it does not agree with the subject *Sui Ky*. Option B is incorrect because it is not a verb form of *write*. Option D is incorrect because it is an incomplete verb form.

22. A. sang

Option A is correct. *Sang* is the past tense of the irregular verb *sing*. Options B and D are incorrect because they do not agree with the subject *Megan*. Option C is incorrect because it is an incomplete verb form.

23. B. fell

Option B is correct. *Fell* is the past tense of the irregular verb *fall*. Options A, C, and D are incorrect because they do not agree with the subject *I*.

24. D. will run

Option D is correct. *Will run* is the future tense of *run*. Option A is incorrect because it is not a verb form of *run*. Options B and C are incorrect because they do not agree with the subject *Jacee*.

Lesson 15 (pages 75–77)

1. B. in chicago

Option B contains an error. *Chicago* is the name of a city, so it is a proper noun. Always capitalize the names of cities and towns. Options A and C are correctly in the past tense. They both describe an action that happened in the past. Option D is incorrect because the sentence does contain an error.

2. D. No error.

Option D is correct. Option A is the correct form of the verb *work*. Options B and C are proper nouns, and they begin with capital letters.

3. A. Ted and I washes

Option A contains an error. The subject is two people *(Ted and I)*; it is a first-person plural subject (like the word *we*). The correct verb form for a first-person plural subject is *wash*. The verb must be in the present tense because it describes an action that is ongoing. Option B is a common noun, so it is not capitalized. Option C uses the correct verb form. Option D is incorrect because the sentence does contain an error.

4. A. I is liking
Option A contains an error. The sentence describes something that is generally true; the regular verb should be in the present tense. The verb also must agree with the first-person subject *I*. Options B and C use verbs correctly. Option D is incorrect because the sentence contains an error.

5. B. pulls out the weeds
Option B contains an error. The subject (*I*) does two things: *water* and *pull*. Both verbs should be in the present tense and must agree with the first-person singular subject *I*. Options A and C are in the present tense because the sentence states facts about ongoing actions. Option D is incorrect because the sentence contains an error.

6. C. Mr. Abdul talk
Option C contains an error. *Mr. Abdul* is the subject of the regular verb *talk*. For regular verbs, the letter -*s* is added to the present tense verb when the subject is the third-person singular. Option A is in the future tense because it describes a future outcome. Option B is not capitalized because *gardens* is a common noun. Option D is incorrect because the sentence contains an error.

7. C. bugs that harms
Option C contains an error. The verb does not agree with the subject. The subject *bugs* is a third-person plural subject. The third-person plural verb form is *harm*. Options A and B have correct subject-verb agreement. Option D is incorrect because the sentence contains an error.

8. C. hoverflies is good
Option C contains an error. *Hoverflies* is the plural subject of a form of the irregular verb *be*. The correct form of the verb is *are*. Option A is the correct capitalization of a proper name and title. Option B is the correct future tense. The words *next week* are a clue that this action takes place in the future. Option D is incorrect because the sentence contains an error.

9. C. dallas
Option C contains an error. *Dallas* is the name of a city, so it is a proper noun. Proper nouns should be capitalized. Options A and B have the correct tense and subject-verb agreement. Option D is incorrect because the sentence contains an error.

10. B. I are
Option B contains an error. The word *I* is the subject of the irregular verb *be*, so the correct form of the verb is *am*. Option A uses the correct verb form. Option C uses the correct capitalization. Option D is incorrect because the sentence contains an error.

11. B. begin
Option B contains an error. The subject *I* has already started the new job. The verb should be in the past tense. The correct form of the irregular verb is *began*. Option A is in the present tense because the family's happiness is ongoing. Option C correctly describes a past action. Option D is incorrect because the sentence contains an error.

12. A. We move
Option A contains an error. The correct verb form is past tense. Option A should be *We moved*. In option B, the name of the month, *August,* is correctly capitalized. Option C is in the past tense. The word *before* tells you that this past action happened before the other past action of moving. Option D is incorrect because the sentence contains an error.

13. C. practice
Option C contains an error. The sentence describes events in the past. Both verbs (*took* and *practice*) should be in the past tense. The past tense of *practice* that agrees with the subject is *practiced*. Options A and B do not contain errors. Option D is incorrect because the sentence contains an error.

14. A. The stack of invoices sit
Option A contains an error. The simple subject of the sentence is *stack*. (Remember not to let words that separate a subject and a verb confuse you.) The correct verb form is *sits*. Options B and C do not contain an error. Option D is incorrect because the sentence contains an error.

15. B. when you met
Option B contains an error. The verb *met* is past tense, which is incorrect. It follows the time word *when,* so the verb should be in the present tense (*meet*). Option A is future tense because the question asks about a future action. Option C is in the present tense because the verb follows the time word *after,* so the verb is present tense *leave*. Option D is incorrect because the sentence contains an error.

16. B. I are telling
Option B contains an error. The verb *are* does not agree with the subject *I*. Also, the verb should be past tense. The correction is *I told*. Options A and C have the correct tense and subject-verb agreement. Also, in option C the proper noun *Lou* is correctly capitalized.

Option D is incorrect because the sentence contains an error.

17. A. pile of dirty clothes are
Option A contains an error. The subject of option A, *pile,* is singular. The action is in the present tense. The correct verb form for the third-person singular is *is*. Options B and C are correctly in the present tense. Option D is incorrect because the sentence does contain an error.

18. A. I surprised
Option A contains an error. The verb should be the future tense form, *I will surprise*. Option B is present tense because it comes after the time word *when*. Option C contains no error. Option D is incorrect because the sentence does contain an error.

Check In 2 (pages 79–83)

1. A. Destiny
Option A is correct. *Destiny* names the person who parked the car. Option B is incorrect because *car* tells what she parked. Option C is incorrect because *grocery* tells what kind of store. Option D is incorrect because *store* names the place near which Destiny parked the car.

2. C. grill
Option C is correct. The word *grill* names the thing that Carl stores in the garage. Option A is incorrect because *Carl* is the person who stores the grill. Option B is incorrect because *gas* tells what kind of grill it is. Option D is incorrect because *garage* tells where the grill is stored.

3. C. hesitated
Option C is correct. The word *hesitated* means "waited because you were undecided, or felt that you shouldn't"; given Seth's part-time salary, he may feel unsure about buying expensive tickets. Option A is incorrect because *inquired* means "asked"; Seth is not asking about spending money for tickets. Options B and D are incorrect because *insist* means "to refuse to give in" and *celebrate* means "to rejoice"; it is unlikely that Seth would insist on or celebrate spending $90 for a ticket, given his part-time salary.

4. D. offended
Option D is correct. The word *offended* means "upset, or insulted," a likely reaction if you feel ignored. Options A, B, and C are incorrect because *relieved* means "to feel free from troubles," *satisfied* means "contented," and *pleased* means "to feel joy or satisfaction." It is unlikely that Juanita would feel relieved, satisfied, or pleased, since she has received no response from her teacher.

5. A. Don't *lean* against that freshly painted wall.

Option A is correct. *Lean* is used as an action word meaning "to rest your body against something for support." Option B is incorrect because it uses *lean* to mean "to rely upon." Option C is incorrect because it uses *lean* to mean "to agree with or support." Option D is incorrect; it uses *lean* to mean "slim or thin."

6. B. Some breeds of dogs *shed* more than others.

Option B is correct. *Shed* is used as an action word meaning "to lose part of the body as a normal process." Option A is incorrect because *shed* is used to name a small building used for storage. Option C is incorrect because *shed* is used as an action word meaning "to send out." Option D is incorrect because *shed* is used as an action word meaning "poured out as drops."

7. A. 7 A.M.–8 A.M.

Option A is correct because 7 A.M.–8 A.M. is the time that Step Aerobics classes are held. Options B, C, and D are incorrect because they list times when Step Aerobics classes are not held.

8. D. Saturday

Option D is correct because Open Gym is listed under Saturday on the schedule. Options A, B, and C are incorrect because Open Gym is held only on Saturday.

9. C. on the front office bulletin board

Option C is correct because the note at the bottom of the schedule says to see the front office bulletin board for the schedule of outdoor activities. Options A, B, and D are incorrect because there is no schedule for outdoor activities in those places.

10. D. Tues.–Thurs. 2 P.M.–5 P.M.

Option D is correct because youth leagues are listed in the basketball section; they meet Tuesday–Thursday from 2 P.M.–5 P.M. Options A, B, and C are incorrect because the youth leagues are not scheduled for those times.

11. B. mayor

Option B is correct. *Mayor* is a title that should be capitalized when it comes before the person's name. Option A is incorrect because it is part of the verb and should not be capitalized. Options C and D are incorrect because they are common nouns.

12. A. february

Option A is correct. *February* is the name of the second month of the year and should be capitalized. Options B, C, and D are incorrect because they are common nouns.

13. D. orleans

Option D is correct. New Orleans is the name of a city in Louisiana. Both words in the city's name should be capitalized. Options A and B are common nouns. Option C is incorrect because it is a verb.

14. B. (,)

Option B is correct. The sentence lists three things. A comma separates the items in a list of three or more things. Options A, C, or D are marks that appear only at the end of a sentence.

15. D. (?)

Option D is correct. The sentence is a question. A question mark belongs at the end of the sentence. Option A is a period, which ends a sentence that tells a fact. Option B is a comma, which never ends a sentence. Option C is an exclamation point, which is used to show surprise or strong feelings.

16. B. (,)

Option B is correct. The sentence has a list of four names. A comma separates each item in a list of three or more items. Options A, C, and D are incorrect because they would divide the list and make two sentences. The first sentence would be incomplete.

17. C. play

Option C is correct. The sentence tells a fact, so use the present tense form of the verb. The subject of the sentence is *I*. For correct subject-verb agreement, use the first person singular verb form *play*. Options A, B, and D do not have correct subject-verb agreement.

18. D. is

Option D is correct. The sentence tells a fact, so use the present tense form of the verb. The subject, *Fiona*, is the third-person singular. The correct form of the irregular verb *be* is the verb form *is*. Option A is the plural form of the verb. Option B is the plural past tense form of the verb. Option C is the first-person present tense form of the verb.

19. B. bought

Option B is correct. The words *last week* are a clue that the action happened in the past. *Bought* is the past tense form of the irregular verb *buy*. Option A is the present tense form of the verb. Option C is an incomplete verb form. Option D is the wrong tense and needs a plural subject.

20. C. was

Option C is correct. The sentence describes a past tense state of being. *Picnic basket* is one thing, so it needs the singular past tense form of the verb. Option A is the plural past tense form of the verb. Option B is the plural present tense form of the verb. Option D is the base form of the verb *be*.

21. B. will change

Option B is correct. The sentence describes an event that will happen in the future. The words *in the morning* are a clue that the action has not yet happened. The verb is in the future tense. Option A is the present tense verb form. Option C describes a continuing present action and is also an incomplete verb. Option D describes any time up to the present and is the wrong number for the subject, *Ang*.

22. D. are

Option D is correct. The verb form *are* goes with the first-person plural subject *we*. Option A is the singular present tense form of the verb. *Am* does not agree with a first-person plural subject. Option B is the third-person singular form of the verb. Option C is incorrect because the helping verb *has* belongs with a singular subject, and the tense of the verb shows any time up to now.

23. B. when you is ready

Option B contains an error. The subject of the verb in option B is *you*. For correct subject-verb agreement, the verb should be *are (when you are ready)*. Option A correctly uses the future tense. In option C, *Mrs. Lang's* is capitalized correctly. Option D is incorrect because the sentence contains an error.

24. A. Lourdes carry

Option A contains an error. *Lourdes* is a third-person singular subject. The sentence is in the present tense. The correct verb form is *carries*. Option B is the correct present tense third-person singular form of the verb. Option C has no error. Option D is incorrect because the sentence contains an error.

25. C. newark

Option C contains an error. *Newark* is the name of a city. It should be capitalized. Options A and B do not contain an error. Option D is incorrect because the sentence contains an error.

26. D. No error.

Option D is correct. Options A, B, and C do not contain an error.

27. A. vase of flowers sit

Option A contains an error. The simple subject is *vase*, which is singular. The verb form should be *sits*. The word *flowers* is plural, but it is not the subject. The word *flowers* describes the subject, *vase*. Options B and C are incorrect because they do not contain an error. Option D is incorrect because the sentence contains an error.

28. B. eyes of a starfish is

Option B contains an error. The subject in option B is the plural word *eyes*. The verb form needs to be plural *(are)*. Option A correctly uses the future tense. Option C has no errors. Option D is incorrect because the sentence does contains an error.